UFOs Crop Circles and the Mayan Calendar

A Collection of Articles

By Rob Simone

All rights reserved. This book may not be reproduced in whole or in part without written permission from the author except for brief quotations in articles and reviews.

© Copyright 2007 – Rob Simone

Headroom Publishing

Box 9 Lafayette Hill, PA 19444

(614) 748-9471

© Copyright 2007 – Rob Simone

ISBN – 978-1434809827

UFOs
Crop Circles and
the Mayan Calendar

A Collection of Articles

By
Rob Simone

Cover Photographs – Rob Simone

Drombeg Stones, Ireland, crop circle, UK

Headroom Publishing

Box 9 Lafayette Hill, PA 19444

(614) 748-9471

© Copyright 2007 – Rob Simone

This book is dedicated to the finders and the keepers, but mostly to the seekers.

UFOs
Crop Circles and
the Mayan Calendar

A Collection of Articles

By
Rob Simone

Headroom Publishing

Box 9 Lafayette Hill, PA 19444

(614) 748-9471

© Copyright 2007 – Rob Simone

Table of Contents

UFOs and NASA - The Best Evidence..13

The Sun Ship of Sweden..25

Mysteries of the Middle East..39

The Mayan Calendar Decoded..67

Crop Circles – The Message and the Mechanics..77

UFOs – Past Present and Future..91

The Spirituality of Disclosure..95

The Gods of Babylon
The Societies of the Occult..................................105

Biography..145

Lecture Topics..147

INTRODUCTION

This collection of writings spans *some* of the four-year, around-the-world adventure that took me to the Outback of Australia, the Himalayas in Nepal, through Asia, into the Middle East, to the Great Pyramids at Giza, rediscovering the Ark of the Covenant, exploring mystical dimensions and meeting the Dalai Lama.

Some of these articles appeared in FATE magazine and others are published here for the fist time.

I felt it would lay a foundation to assemble these works together before the complete book of my global adventures, "Beyond All Borders" is published.

Along with stunning photographs and artwork, these books represent real-life explorations to the most sacred places on earth and the phenomenon that surrounds them.

Woven through the broad range of topics covered in this book runs a common thread of human experience that speaks to the real history and potential of mankind.

UFOs Crop Circles The Mayan Calendar and Sacred Places

UFOs and NASA: The Best Evidence

(Images – NASA)

One of the primary goals of the National Aeronautics and Space Administration (NASA) is to discover new life in the universe.

From the many images captured by their cameras and the growing testimony of their astronauts, it seems intelligent life HAS been found and it's trying to discover US.

Mitchell's Testimony

© Rob Simone

Rob Simone and Apollo 14 astronaut Dr. Edgar Mitchell

Dr. Edgar Mitchell, Apollo 14 astronaut, was the sixth man to walk on the Moon. He has spoken out on the subject of UFOs and how the extra-terrestrial issue is handled in some circles of the military and government:

"I have met with credible professionals within two governments who have testified to their own firsthand experiences with close encounters. They include members of military intelligence and government whose official duties involved the extraterrestrial presence. As is expected, they were all bound by strict security oath agreements which prevented them from disclosing any of this."

Mitchell has also stated that military personnel with whom he has spoken have seen actual alien bodies in the course of their duties. Dr. Mitchell appeared as a guest on my talk show recently and I asked him about the continuing cover-up, conspiracy, and truth embargo related to the UFO phenomenon.

He had this to say:

"There has been, as we both know, considerable effort within most governments to suppress this information and to limit what is being said about it. Let's hope that it's coming to an end."

Cooper Sees a UFO Landing

In 1965 Gordon Cooper orbited the planet 22 times on the last single-manned space mission. In 1955 Cooper was stationed at Edwards Air Force Base. While supervising the filming of a new landing facility for F-86 fighter jets, he and his crew observed a disc-shaped craft that hovered close to the ground, then extended three retractable landing gear, and set down near the runway.

The film crew approached and continued filming. Cooper states that the craft then lifted off the ground, retracted its gear, and soared off into the sky. When he developed the film it clearly showed the same event he had witnessed.

The film was then sent to Washington where it was classified and remains so to this day. When asked about the current location of this film and other evidence of UFOs captured by the Air Force, Cooper said that within the government and the military, it was impossible to learn where such documents were sent unless you were directly involved, and he was not.

Rob Simone

Apollo Witness Speaks

I was speaking recently at a conference on the subject of comparative UFO mythology of Asian and Middle Eastern traditions. After the talk an older gentleman approached me and told of his involvement with the Apollo missions as a communications engineer.

His duties were to repair and maintain the two-way radios in the spacesuits used by the astronauts on the lunar surface.

During a training exercise at NASA he overheard a conversation between two astronauts on their in-helmet transmitters. They were talking about a briefing they had the day before about the reality of UFOs.

NASA officials told all the Apollo astronauts about unknown craft that had been seen in space on previous missions and that they were not ours. This briefing was done about two weeks before blast-off so they would have time to adjust to this new reality and prevent any panic if and when they saw alien spacecraft during their mission.

NASA most likely gave them instructions on how to handle their radio communications and photography in the event of a sighting.

It would seem NASA secretly briefed most if not all of the Apollo astronauts.

To this day some will only talk about it "off the record."

The Evidence

The photographic evidence NASA has released is even more compelling.

(NASA)

For instance, in this photograph taken on Apollo 15, the view of lunar module at the Hadley Apennine landing site is unusual, not because of what is there, but because of what's missing.

While poring over the thousands of photos at Johnson Space Center in Houston, I came across this image and it caught my eye. The entire top portion of the photo has been cut off, obscuring the upper portion of the spacecraft and the hill and sky behind it.

What could have been so secret to require crudely doctoring this particular image?

Perhaps the reports of multiple UFOs hovering near the Apollo landing sites are true.

In the next photo, we see evidence of what could be ancient alien ruins on the surface of the Moon. In this rarely seen NASA image we see the lunar surface with very clear, sharply pointed shadows extending from what appear to be high mountains.

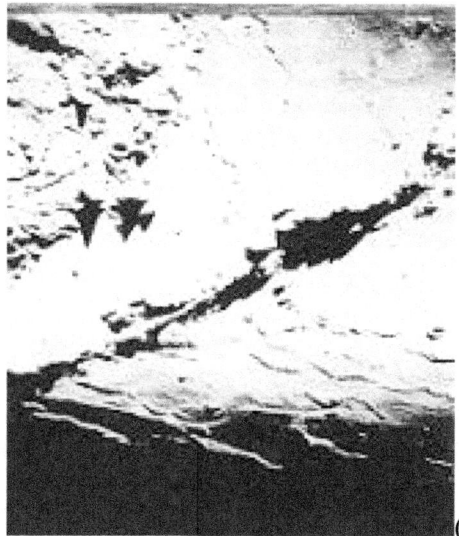
(NASA)

On closer inspection I have noticed that whatever is making these extremely symmetrical shadows is in contrast to the rough and jagged shadows that appear everywhere else. It must be a mountain of unusual height and shape. Moreover, three together suggests an artificial quality similar to the three pyramids at Giza.

If these shadows appeared on Earth, it would be easier to believe they were man-made, but on the Moon, our conditioned response prevents us from considering a broader explanation.

Possible artificial structures have been photographed on the surface of Mars as well. At right, bottom, is the official NASA photograph file # 80-35077 taken by Viking 1 orbiter on July 25, 1976, from a distance of 1,162 miles. Viking 1 was photographing areas in the northern hemisphere looking for possible landing sites for Viking 2.

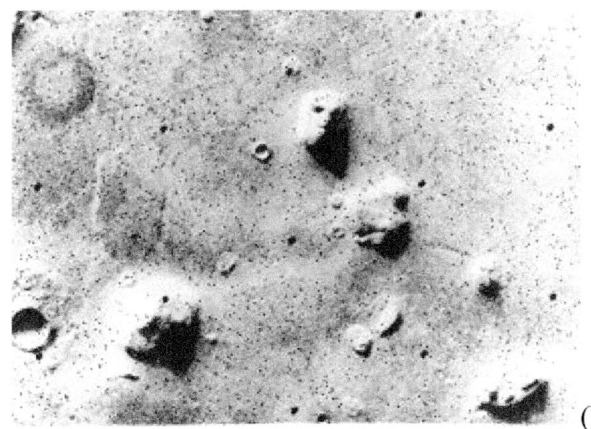

(NASA)

The official explanation for the face-like appearance of this mile-wide rock formation is simply a shadow effect.

The varying degrees of darkness are not uncommon when the sun is at an angle of 20 degrees, as it is in this photograph. The most compelling aspect of this face from the shadows is that also clearly detectable are the mouth, nose, teeth, and a symmetrical head gear feature that runs vertically along the right side of the face.

There is much more to the evidence of artificial structures on the Martian surface. These photos are merely a highlight. Faced with this data it would stand to reason that NASA and the Jet Propulsion Laboratory (the organization responsible for unmanned missions) would turn their attention to these remarkable outcroppings. Instead, only a few more images have been released, and only after relentless public pressure. Some of these were put through a filter that makes the details more difficult to see.

A very rare newspaper clipping shows a 1965 photograph from the Soviet Zond-3 spacecraft. It seems to show a disc-shaped craft orbiting the Moon.

UFOs Crop Circles The Mayan Calendar and Sacred Places

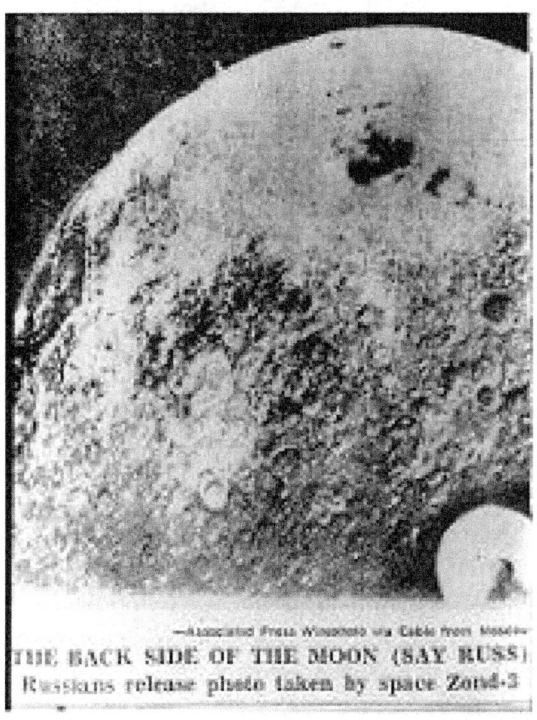

THE BACK SIDE OF THE MOON (SAY RUSS) Russians release photo taken by space Zond-3

What struck me about this photo were the shape and features of the UFO. I knew I had seen this one before, but where?

I searched through my collection of UFO pictures from around the world until I found the picture with the craft that looked exactly the same.

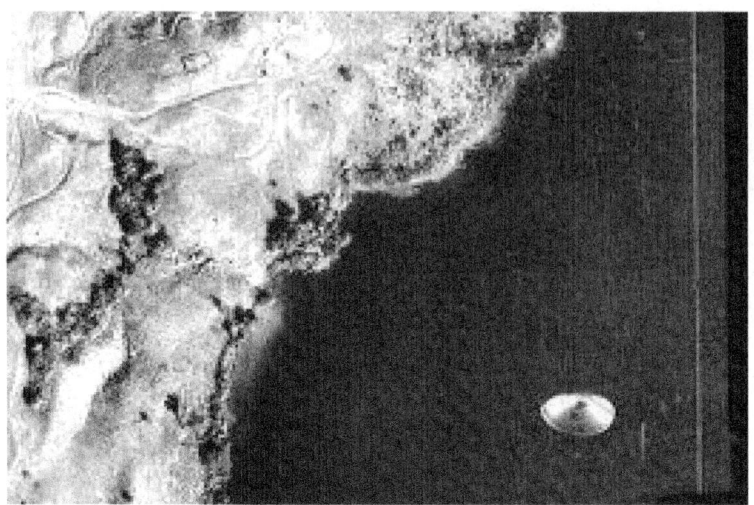

This picture shows a striking similarity to the UFO in the Russian shot. It was taken by an official mapping aircraft of the Costa Rican government on September 4, 1971, while flying at 10,000 feet altitude over a body of water known as Lago de Cote.

The Costa Rican image appears on the cover of the Cometa report, a briefing document by the French space agency and military advisors stating that someUFOs have to be extraterrestrial in origin. They chose this picture because it is virtually indisputable.

In the back of my mind I seemed to recall yet another photograph with the same UFO.

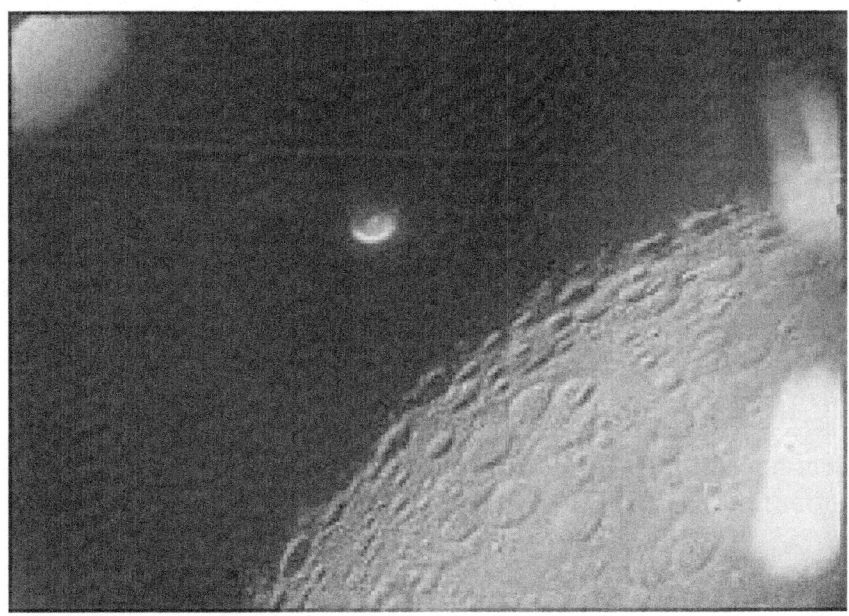

This photograph, from Apollo 16 in 1972, on the approach to the moon seems to show a UFO with the same characteristics.

Could this be evidence of a craft intent on being pictured multiple times?

Perhaps it is part of a fleet of spacecraft that circled the Earth and Moon 30 years ago.

Time for Disclosure

The few pieces of evidence that have filtered down into the public domain are most likely a small fraction of photos kept in classified files within the governments of the world. I have been collecting these pictures in the hopes of presenting them in this and future articles to offer some perspective and understanding to this perplexing field of study.

Rob Simone

It is my hope that the area of ET contact, both now and in ancient times, might become part of a normal course of study at colleges and universities.

The emerging science of Ufology may hold solutions to ongoing religious and political unrest that serves only to polarize humanity. It could be that the widespread disclosure of ET reality could unify the world in a way that nothing else could.

The importance of this subject is among the highest as it impacts our society, our faith, and our fundamental understanding of the universe in which we live.

UFOs Crop Circles The Mayan Calendar and Sacred Places

The Sun Ship of Sweden

© Rob Simone

Sweden is best known for its clean culture, safe cars and IKEA.

It's also where you can find one of the world's most amazing stone circles.

I left London, where I used to live, to visit a friend in Sweden, a country that had no mystical places to explore, or so I thought...

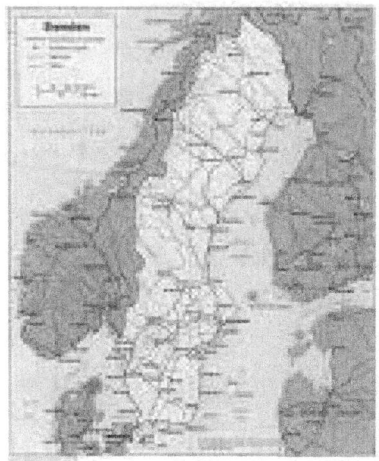

Never having been there, I was unsure of what Sweden would be like and as I boarded the train to Göteborg from Copenhagen, I was filled with a sense of blind anticipation.

Having just finished a three year journey of many of the sacred sites around the world, I had become accustomed to automatically seeking out the most mystical places in any new land.

As soon as I arrived at the train station, I started asking around if there were any monolithic structures in the country.

Everybody I asked said there was no such thing in Sweden. Disappointed, I decided to go to Lund, a very old city, to do some routine sightseeing.

Lund was founded in 1000 AD and is the second oldest town in Sweden. Preferring to stay at a variety of accommodations, I ended up in a hostel that had been converted from several boxcar trains. The reception desk was in one of the conductor's compartments and things were a bit cramped. The man who worked there was a very spiritual person and liked to get to know every one and offer advice, not just the usual tourist information, but advice on life as well.

I would come to find out he was a sort of a… hostel owner/guru/train conductor guy.

Once I was settled in I went to ask him about the local points of interest. We ended up having a two-hour philosophical discussion about the nature of the universe.

I seem to find people to talk about these kinds of things wherever I go. As I was leaving I happened to see a picture of a massive stone circle pinned on the bulletin board next to the reception desk. I asked him what that was.

He told me that it was a megalithic structure in a remote, southern part of Sweden near a city called Ystad and it was a very special place.

He had spent time in the area several years ago and had even taken part in a spiritual ceremony near the circle.

With a slight smile he said, "You should go there for the experience, you seem to have the right energy for that place."

"Does it have a name?" I asked.

"Yes, it's called the Sun Ship."

I left the next day.

During the train ride to Ystad I kept thinking about what the hostel owner/guru/train conductor guy told me.

He said I should go for "the experience", but it seemed he meant it not as a thing to do, but rather as a specific event that somehow he had future knowledge of. It was as if he entered my life simply to point me to this powerful and ancient site.

The name of the circle also intrigued me: The Sun Ship.

The sun ship is well known in Egyptian mythology.

The Sun-God Ra sailed from East to West every day on the beams of the sun in a "ship" of his making.

In Greek mythology there are specific references to northern races and sun gods.

One myth speaks of the "Hyperboreans," as they were called, who lived "up in the north," in a land of unbroken sunshine at the edge of the world. Apollo himself was said to spend his winters in this land.

They were also known to worship the "White Swan" which is believed to be the messenger of the Sun God.

UFOs Crop Circles The Mayan Calendar and Sacred Places

As I drew nearer to the town of Ystad my expectations were soaring.

I only had rough directions and I ended up in a place beyond the reach of busses or trains.

I hitched a few rides and made my way to a very rural, farm country and began a four hour trek through crop fields, back roads and finally to the coast line.

I knew the circle was right on the edge of the ocean, so walking along the beach was the surest way to find it.

Finally I saw what looked like a giant crown set in the hillside off in the distance.

As I drew near, it was a spectacle to see the stones slowly rise from the land in front of me. With each step the stones grew higher until I reached the top of the cliff and stared in awe at their precision and grandeur.

© Rob Simone

The circle is 1,500 years old and made up of 59 massive boulders stretching over 65 meters long and 19 meters wide. They sit on a cliff on the ocean's edge, which offers an un-obscured 180° view of the southern sky.

This allowed the ancient people to track the course of the sun as it rose and set. The ancient builders erected these 3-ton megaliths in exact locations marking the sun's position during the winter and summer solstices and equinox orbit points.

© Rob Simone

It is said that if you place a 11-foot pole at the right angle in the middle of the circle, you can make a "sun dial" to tell time and mark the passing hours.

The two end stones, which are three times as big as the other stones, were mined and transported there from a location many miles away.

UFOs Crop Circles The Mayan Calendar and Sacred Places

© Rob Simone

They are positioned with such accuracy that even today they can track each hour and day of a solar year.

This feat alone would have been a major undertaking for that time and demonstrates the profound importance of the exact construction of this site.

For reasons still unknown, the builders ignored the rocks that were very close by. There was sufficient material to mine but it was deemed unsuitable, which only deepens the mystery of the circle.

I spent all day there walking around, taking measurements and trying to imagine how it looked a thousand years ago.

I decided to spend the night and watch the stars revolve around me in order to experience exactly what the original inhabitants would have seen.

It was July in Sweden, which meant the sun would go down at 11:00 p.m. or later. Just after midnight the circle fell into a primordial darkness.

There was only the sound of the motion of the waves and the creatures stirring in the distance.

© Rob Simone

I was utterly alone, yet profoundly at peace.

I decided to attempt a metaphysical exploration of this sacred place.

Drawing upon my training in India, I began to ready myself for an out-of-body experience.

The conditions were right. It was warm, quiet and I could lie in the middle of the circle and focus on leaving the confines of my physical body and allow my spirit to navigate the astral plane.

After an hour of lying there, the strangest thing happened. I saw what looked like the letter "**R**" somehow take shape from the uneven edges of the stone right in front of me.

As my first name is Rob I though it was my own ego tricking me, but then I felt a strange sensation, like my body was growing and I was 20 feet long. When I opened my eyes the sensation would leave.

Once again after some mediation, this feeling retuned with a sense of spinning and falling. Since I was alone out there, I felt it best to stop and try sleeping instead.

It turned out to be the right choice.

What happened next was an incredible experience. To this day I still can't say if it was real or a very vivid and lucid dream.

I awoke to sound of people approaching the cliff. In the dead of night and at such a remote location this seemed very strange. What was even stranger was the *kind* of sounds they were making.

I heard people talking but not in Swedish, it was a more guttural sounding dialect. There were also the sounds of heavy footsteps and metal banging together as if they had loosely tied various objects to the backs of pack animals.

Then almost instantly they were all around me. Tall dark figures assembled all around the circle.

As amazed as I was to see this I knew on some level that this stone circle belong to them and they were there for some sort of ceremony.

I found myself facing the tallest figure that was holding a staff of some sort.

He gestured to me to come closer and as I did, the crowd parted and they began to enter the circle as I stood off in the distance. They moved in a solemn deliberate way.

They began to tie ropes around the entire diameter of the circle and erect what looked to be a wooden sail in the middle. It was as if the stones were a real vessel and they were preparing to set sail.

Rob Simone

© Rob Simone

All of the figures were beginning to activate the circle somehow.

I took a few steps closer and began thinking how I could communicate my intentions for peaceful interaction when all of a sudden I was among them, inside the circle, looking at them trying to see their faces when the sky caught my eye.

Instead of seeing the familiar constellations I saw a blur of lights and color. I was transfixed. Suddenly it stopped. I thought it was only my imagination until I looked outside the circle. The cliff and the ocean were gone!

Now as I looked out to the countryside it was a completely different place.

I could see high mountains and vast plains. As I struggled to make out a temple type structure off in the distance, I noticed that there were figures coming in and out of the circle. It was as if we docked to let people on and off the ship!

This happened two more times, each with a different landscape and then, all of a sudden, we were back by the sea.

As the figures started to leave the circle and take down the ropes, I looked for the tall one that had gestured toward me. He was standing next to one of the large end stones and as I approached him he reached out to hand me something. Just as I looked down to see what was in my hands, I found myself alone, cold, and very thirsty in the middle of the circle.

I couldn't think clearly, I was completely exhausted and quickly fell asleep.

As for the letter "**R**" I saw in the rock just before the journey, it seems there is more to it.

The ancient script language of Scandinavia is called " Runes" which are used for writing, divination and magic. There is one Rune that looks exactly like the letter" **R**" and it's called "Raido."

This is the same symbol I saw in the uneven edges of the rock that night.

The fact that it has the same letters as the word "radio", and I host a radio show is interesting. Even more interesting is that it is considered the "rune of journeys". Since I had just been on an incredible ride, I thought this couldn't be a coincidence.

When I looked up this particular Rune, I was amazed to discover the significance of this symbol as it relates to traveling adventures.

The Raido Rune warns us that there is no shortcut to the end of our journey. Taking the easy way out is a false solution and does not lead to a meaningful conclusion.

We must be prepared to embrace new experiences in life. It is held by many that our time on this planet is no more than preparation for the next life, and it's important to travel wisely; to learn and understand what you can on this earthly plane of existence while there is time.

In Rune magic, Raido is used as protection for vehicles and travelers. It is the least ambiguous of all the runes and it is the easiest to invoke in charms and spells.

Raido is also called "right action" which further peaked my interest.

I have been painting calligraphy ever since I spent time in Japan.

One of the first symbols I learned is one called "yi" or "right choice."

(Artwork by Rob Simone)

The meaning of the calligraphy is almost identical to the Raido Rune.

The Next Journey

I left the circle and headed north toward Stockholm.

One of other amazing features of the Sun Ship is its perfect alignment with other stone structures many miles away.

Several days later I came upon another megalithic site that had the same markings and design as the sun ship.

It was smaller in scale, yet it still had the precise angles of light and shadow that correspond with the summer and winter solstice.

The two end stones were very close together and just a bit shorter than eye level. I began to collect some scientific data from the area.

I started taking field strength measurements along the standard electromagnetic spectrums and discovered there was a strong magnetic anomaly at the point pictured in the photograph.

© Rob Simone

The North Pole indicator on my compass would "bend" consistently 33° off center every time I came to that spot.

Whether the two end stones pictured are the source of this disturbance, or there is something buried under the site is still not known.

I have since traveled throughout Ireland and the U.K. exploring and cataloging many more stone circles. The similarity of the astrological significance of stone structures in different countries has always fascinated me, but the energy anomalies associated with some of these ancient sites suggests to me that further research beyond the conventional approach is necessary.

I suspect there is a direct connection between the strange magnetic readings and the construction of this site and other stone circles around the world.

UFOs Crop Circles The Mayan Calendar and Sacred Places

Mysteries of the Middle East

© Rob Simone

In all my travels around the world, the regions of Turkey, Israel, and Egypt were by far the most powerful and mysterious.

Rob Simone

Abydos

Egypt is well known for its pyramids, tombs, temples, and ancient cities.
But there is a place that was sacred long before any of these things ever existed.

After traveling halfway around the world from Japan to India, I made my way through Petra in Jordan, boarding a ship from Aquaba on the southern coast, to the Sinai Peninsula.

I watched the sunset from the top of Mt. Sinai, where Moses received the Ten Commandments, then continued onward in my quest to explore the sacred places of the past.

© Rob Simone

From the peninsula I traveled overland through southern Egypt and Luxor, where I heard from an old man who guarded the entrance of one of the tombs in the Valley of the Kings about a little town called

Abydos to the north, which holds the greatest mystery.

Getting off the microbus on the highway next to the road to Abydos, I started walking toward the town when two heavily armed soldiers told me to stop, and that I was not permitted to continue.

I ignored them, thinking that they knew I was a foreigner, and were trying to pressure me for money.

Looking around and seeing everyone else able to go about their business, I continued on, and again they insisted I stop.

I finally acknowledged them and told them I was going to walk in to town. They said, "Not possible". I pulled out my passport and flipped through the many stamps and permits until I got to my Egyptian visa. I showed it to them, saying, "See this? This allows me to go anywhere in Egypt."

They stood their ground but did not get angry, in fact, they were more polite than I was accustomed to. I realized they were acting in my best interest.

We walked to the guardhouse at the corner, and there it was explained that the rest of the distance to Abydos could only be traveled if an armed guard escorted me. Seeing no other option, I was joined by two AK-47-clad soldiers in an old Peugot station-wagon taxi for the next ten miles of dusty, desert road.

No other place in Egypt requires this level of security. Unlike most of Egypt, which is very safe, the area around Abydos is known to harbor extreme Muslim fundamentalists who won't hesitate to kill or kidnap foreign travelers, especially Americans.

At least this is what I was told.

When we arrived in Abydos, the soldiers walked, ate, and slept wherever I did. They were part of a platoon of other soldiers stationed there and had an armored attack vehicle parked right outside my sleeping quarters. How comforting!

© Rob Simone

On my first day there I met an older European woman in an electric wheelchair next to the temple. She had lived in Abydos for many years and believed the area held an energy that heals the body and cures disease. She was diagnosed with terminal cancer and given eight months to live.

That was ten years ago!

The existence of such special energetic properties might explain why Abydos has been Egypt's premier pilgrimage site for more than 3,000 years.

In ancient times, Abydos was a holy center where pharaohs and commoners joined in festivals and ceremonies in honor of the gods, especially Osiris, ruler of the Egyptian underworld.

The Abydos temple has seven sanctuaries dedicated to different deities: Ra, Amun-Ra, Ptah, Ra-Harakhty, Horus, Isis, and Osiris.

Immediately behind the chambers dedicated to the Osiris cult, is another structure, a subterranean temple called the Osireion.

It contains offering scenes and other items from the Book of the Dead.

I was able to spend all day and night in and around the temple, looking at every hieroglyph and feature of this amazing place.

© Rob Simone

There were no other foreigners there, so the guards let me go anywhere I wanted.
I wanted to go where no other foreigners were allowed.

One area I studied was the "Corridor of Kings" which named all the kings of Abydos from the beginning of time. On the opposite wall was a list of all the gods of Egypt.

Their reign spanned some 40,000 years, putting the true timeline of this ancient place in question. This suggests a far older legacy than that which is believed by established archaeology.

© Rob Simone

The town of Abydos is quite small, and I quickly made friends with the locals and was able to gain more insight into this remarkable place. I was told that of a secret library, known only to the guardians, within the walls of the temple.

The library's contents are said to reveal the secrets of the Osireion. This shrine predates the temple and has been continually flooded since its discovery, preventing any real exploration even with modern technology.

Perhaps this is the reason for all the soldiers in this very small town. Does the Osireion hold some great secret?

Dorothy Eady, better known as Omm Sety, spent the better part of her life studying the Abydos temple (1933 to 1981), and had this to say about the Osireion:

"This imposing subterranean building is one of the great puzzles of Egyptian archaeology. No one really knows who built it or for what purpose, and so far as is known, there is not another one like it in the whole of Egypt. It would seem as though some Egyptians regarded it as the Tomb of Osiris. But as the channel surrounding the island has never yet been freed of its water, despite the use of powerful pumps, and probably never will be, it will always remain one of the most breathtaking puzzles of Egyptology."

© Rob Simone

I was able to develop a friendly relationship with the guards, and they allowed me special access to the flooded ruin. The stone blocks demonstrated a different building technique than the temple, and the ever-present water seems to be a fail-safe mechanism to ensure that what is down there remains undisturbed.

That is what I was told by one of my guards, who went on to say that he had witnessed a tidal rhythm which peaks in the spring and wanes in the summer.

© Rob Simone

During one low point he witnessed a vision on the surface of the water that appeared to be a map. On further investigation, he found the lines were carved in the ceiling of one of the supporting columns and only visible as a reflection on the water's surface at midday during a low tide.

© Rob Simone

He began to draw the map in the sand and explained that the two lines represented the two peaks in the distance and the circles a time of celestial alignment which would trigger an opening of the Osireion so that the rest of the flooded temple could be explored and the remaining hieroglyphs be translated, which could finally reveal the secrets of the temple of Abydos.

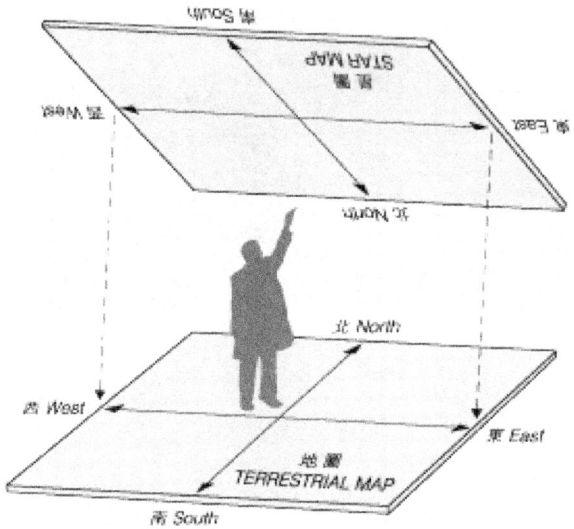

At first I thought my informant could be imagining everything; perhaps he'd spent too many days out in the desert sun. On further investigation I became aware of who he actually was. Not only was he a guard, he was a former curator of the Egyptian Museum in Cairo!

During the next few weeks I remained at Abydos and continued to explore this magical site.

There are hieroglyphics in the temple unlike any others in Egypt. I tried to photograph the "map reflection", but due to the limitations of my camera, it was difficult.

The date of which my guide spoke is approaching in the next few years.

I plan to return to Abydos with selected field researchers and archaeologists.

Perhaps we will witness the next chapter of history, literally rising to surface to shed new light on one of Egypt's most mysterious places.

The Fires of Mt. Olimpos

From Egypt I traveled to Turkey. It was my second time in the country, and I was looking forward to returning.

I decided to travel along the southern coast, which has many beautiful beaches and Roman ruins. I stopped at a hotel in a place called Olimpos.

The rooms were in tree houses around a central fire pit where the guests would gather in the evenings to talk and sing.

One night I overheard another guest talking about a place not far away in the mountains where fire comes from the rocks. That sounded like my kind of place. The following night some other travelers and I set out to see for ourselves if the legends of the eternal flames of Mt. Olimpos were true.

Olimpos is a pre-Greek word for the mountain that was the home of the gods in Greek mythology

Olimpos is first mentioned in the records of history in 78 BC., when the Roman governor Servilius Vatia defeated the clan of pirates who controlled the mountain. It's been said that these pirates used the fires to make strange sacrifices to the Persian god Mithras.

Alexander the Great used this area as a stronghold in the early stages of his conquest of the ancient world.

Mt. Olimpos is known locally as "Chimera," which in ancient legend was a fire-breathing monster with the head of a lion, the body of a goat, and a serpent's tail.

We made our way north from the coast relying of the directions of passersby.

Just after sunset we came to the foot of the mountain and started to climb. We were encouraged to see evidence of previous explorers, a crude path and the odd sign, and finally we could smell a distinct odor overpowering the strong pine scent, which filled the night air.

The tree line was almost below us and we were now challenged with sheer rocks and boulders to scale in the pitch darkness. As we made our way to a clearing, a faint glow caught my eye.

The strange glow grew brighter as we approached, until reddish-blue flames spewing from every rock surrounded us.

© Rob Simone

It was strange to see such an inferno with no wood or fuel, only the smallest crack in the rock.

The fires have been burning for thousands of years, and remain home to the gods of legend to locals and historians.

Warmed by the eternal flame I made my way down the mountain on to the next adventure: Israel.

The Cave of Christ

© Rob Simone

Israel is a beautifully dangerous land of contrasts. I arrived during the last intifadah, an uprising by the Palestinian Arabs in the Gaza Strip and West Bank. This made my journey difficult, because that's exactly where I was headed.

Bethlehem is in the West Bank. To get there you have to ride the minibuses with the Palestinians who go back and forth from Jerusalem. Often checkpoints and violence make this trip difficult and risky.

I was determined to see the Cave of the Nativity, about which I had heard so much from authors and historians. This ancient site has been long believed to be the actual location of the birth of Christ.

The Emperor Constantine built a basilica on the cave site. It is the oldest Christian church in the world.

Rob Simone

After making it through multiple checkpoints, we passed through the border, which brought a big sigh of relief, as I had no visa to enter this part of Israel. Bearing some resemblance to my fellow passengers might have made the difference. Palestine is a place where people are used to hardships, and danger is a normal part of everyday life.

When I arrived in Bethlehem, the church was deserted, and I was able to soak in the magnitude of this holy place alone. The church itself is large and open.

No services were taking place; there were only a few armed Palestinian police standing guard.

To see the cave, I approached the back of the church and went down two levels.

The guards looked me over, a bit surprised to see a visitor in such a dangerous time. They allowed me to pass, and I descended the stairs through an ornate passageway to the cave.

The religious artifacts and ornamentation surrounding the cave appeared to be thousands of years old.

A silver star that surrounds a small hole in the stone adorned the actual place of Christ's birth.

The power of this place was overwhelming. I have personally heard stories of men having to be carried out of there after being overcome with emotion.

UFOs Crop Circles The Mayan Calendar and Sacred Places

© Rob Simone

Visiting this shrine, in the shadow of such conflict made me realize the importance of Christ's message and the irony of the current state of his birthplace.

The bus ride back to Jerusalem was more eventful. After noticing an Israeli checkpoint ahead, our driver swerved off the main road through a maze of residential streets.

This can't be good, I thought.

Perhaps the driver was wanted by the Israeli army and was about to become even more desperate.

It soon became clear he was attempting to not only bypass the checkpoint, for reasons unknown, but was also hiding from the surveillance cameras, which are affixed to many of the buildings and telephone poles.

We soon ended up in a war-torn area covered in rubble and burned-out cars.

I was more worried about what the Israeli army might do to us if we were caught than our overzealous driver.

Having successful avoided the checkpoints, our driver resumed his normal route.

We made it back onto the main road, and once inside Jerusalem I got out and walked the rest of the way, relieved and still reeling from the experience of being in such a holy place.

© Rob Simone

That night I bought a bottle of wine for 13 shekels and joined the other travelers on the roof of the Petra Hotel. The open roof makes all of the sacred places in Jerusalem visible like nowhere else in the city: the Church of the Holy Sepulchre, believed to be the site where Jesus was crucified and buried; the Wailing Wall; the Mount of Olives; and the Dome of the Rock.

The Dome of the Rock is built on what is considered to be the foundation stone of the world. This is where the Prophet Mohammed ascended into heaven, and where Abraham committed the supreme act of faith on God's instructions by offering to sacrifice his son Isaac.

It's also the site where Jacob saw the ladders ascending into heaven.

On this night, the Dome of the Rock was going to amaze us all with a new mystery, one never before seen.

The Shadow of the Dome

At about ten o'clock there were nine or so travelers on the roof, some who had lived at the hotel for years. I approached the railing and gazed out over the lights of the city, reflecting on the day's events.

I was in deep contemplation over the grand traditions of the three religions that lay claim to this land, and the overwhelming sorrow caused by the endless conflict that surrounds the holy sites, when my eye caught something strange emanating from the top of the Dome of the Rock: a shadow!

There was a black beam from the apex of the dome went all the way up to the sky.

No trick of light, this, there was too much light pollution from the rest of the city to account for shadow.

When I called the others to see it, they were all stunned. We spent the rest of the night in awe of this bewildering beam.

Taking several photos, I was sure there was some explanation for this, but the darkness of the shadow and the height it reached in the sky make me think there is another reason for this event.

© Rob Simone

enhanced

The dome covers a large rock where according to scholars, the Profit Mohammed ascended into heaven, lying the foundation for one of the world's fastest growing religions, Islam.

It is also said to be the "foundation stone" of the world, meaning when god made the earth, this spot was made first.

It is also the location where the story of Jacobs saw the "ladders" ascending into heaven.

Could this be an actual photograph of Jacob's Ladder?

The shadow only appeared on certain nights, yet the lighting in the city was always the same. It may be glimpse of some metaphysical energy relating to the biblical accounts.

Faith may once again hold the answers our rational mind can't grasp.

To this day this phenomenon has not been explained. Perhaps when I return, more can be understood about this and the other mysteries of the Middle East.

UFOs Crop Circles The Mayan Calendar and Sacred Places

2012 and the Mayan Calendar Decoded

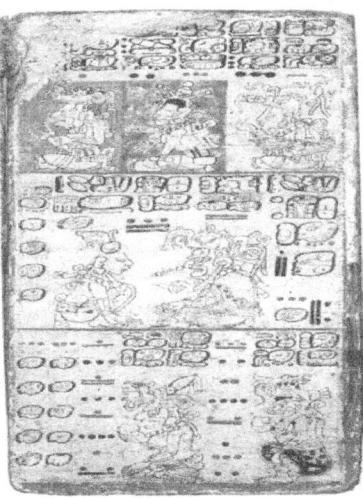

The most accurate observations of the planets and the stars have produced the most accurate device of measuring and predicting their movements and cycles. The honor of the first great civilization to achieve this milestone was not the Egyptians or the Greeks; it was the Mayans, over 2000 years ago.

As many people know the Mayan calendar is one of the most precise almanacs ever devised. Many people in many different areas of academia and philosophy reference the ending of the calendar on December 21, 2012.

It's not entirely accurate to say that it "ends," for the calendar has truly no beginning or ending. It's more precise to say that the calendar tracks the circular movements of the planets and stars and several major cycles that come to a conclusion on December 21, which is the winter solstice.

Further, according the U.S Naval Observatory's Astronomical Applications Dept. the exact time of the Solstice on December 21st 2012 will be 11:11 am!

This is interesting as many people report seeing the numbers 11:11 at strange times and places, and there is a growing belief that it is a trigger of some sort. I, and many other people, have seen this on digital clocks after a random urge to check the time.

This grand cycle of history that ends in 2012 will have lasted for 5,125 years and has and will greatly affect the earth and its people. This time period represents the present "history of civilization."

The grand cycle measures the earth's rotation in and out of the middle point of the Milky Way's density mass. The Mayans recorded the path of the stars over long periods of observation, and calculated when the plane of the ecliptic would be conjoined with the earth and sun.

This area is far more energized with what astronomers call "dark matter" and could therefore dramatically interact with the earth's magnetic field and human physiology.

The extent and range of this influence is unknown, but I maintain it will energize dormant energy systems in all living matter and in the earth itself.

The Mayans recognized the magnitude of this grand cycle of alignment and counted backwards to mark its beginning on August 11, 3114 BC.

The Ancient Measure of Time

Evidence of calendars has been found as far back as 30,000 B.C. during the Paleolithic period. They were represented as regular notches on the horns of bison and animal tusks, which indicated a record of lunar cycles and other celestial observations.

The tree calendar, or moon calendar of the ancient Druids has thirteen moons and twenty-eight day cycles, which is similar to the Incan calendar and can also be found in Polynesia and virtually every other ancient civilization on every continent.

In ancient times, when humans lived closer to earth, maintaining the balance with nature was key to their very survival. The calendar was the primary way to achieve this.

The true purpose of time should be to synchronize ourselves with the earth, the living rhythms of our solar system, and the universe.

Rob Simone

The Gregorian Calendar – Decreed, not Discerned

Our current means of measuring time is artificial.

During the sixteenth century Pope Gregory XIII decreed that, because their current calendar was continually inaccurate and caused religious holidays to move more and more out of date, this demanded a "leap year" be added and other revisions be made.

This arbitrary means of calculating days and years is not in alignment with the true movements of the planets and the sun. This causes everyone who follows this calendar to be disconnected from the natural rhythms of the universe.

Turning our backs on the movement and alignments of the planets, something that all of the ancient civilizations held dear, causes us to be off center in our day-to-day and year-to-year planning. Our understanding of ourselves and our relationship with time itself is also negatively affected.

The byproduct of living in artificial time is entropy of vision and consciousness. The easiest way out of this dilemma is the use of the Mayan calendar, which is more a measure of synchronicity, and puts us in a natural harmonic cadence with all the other cycles of cosmic consciousness.

The Mayan concept of time is the universal factor of synchronization, which opens us up telepathically on a continual basis, rather than just random events as it is now.

The "cloud" of false time and false concepts makes it very difficult for synchronicity to penetrate our consciousness. Whatever your idea of God is, or your faith or religion, we can all agree on the important significance of the orbits and rotation cycles of our solar system.

They provide us with information on the seasons, planting crops, harvesting, and many other vital human components. It is easy to imagine that using a measurement of time, which is completely organic in its creation and corresponds to the natural rotations of the heavenly bodies and affects us directly in the form of light, shadow, and gravity, would be more natural and more understandable to us on a rational and intuitive level.

On the whole planet, the only species not living in harmony with the rest of the universe are humans. Some of the problems that plague mankind, such as war and greed, can all be traceable back to our use and creation of this artificial time.

Truly, the use of the Gregorian calendar marks man's deviation from nature. With our backs turned to the environment, mankind has laid a foundation for the overwhelming and critical environmental disaster, which now threatens humans on every part of the earth.

From around the time of the birth of Christ, the Mayan civilization demonstrated a remarkable rate of development. It seems apparent, however, that the Mayans possessed the calendar as early as 200 B.C. In 400 A.D. they constructed many temple cities, which reflected a very sophisticated level of design. They lived under what could best be described as a theocracy, and at their peak, were using up to nineteen different calendars, which demonstrates their sophisticated understanding of time.

The reason for the different cycles in the Mayan calendar was to measure specific stars and planets such as the Pleiades, Jupiter, Saturn, and the sun. This included the planet Pluto, which was not discovered by Western astronomers until 1930.

This level of sophistication was far more detailed than what is required for simple agricultural use. It is possible that the source of the knowledge of these various cycles did not originate on earth, and was a result of some extra-dimensional influence. Perhaps it was an attempt to establish a "galactic timing standard" for the benefit of humanity.

ANCIENT MAYAN CONTACT

Observation of the stars and planets alone does not fully explain the development of such an advanced calendar. It has been speculated that extra-terrestrial visitors were responsible in giving this information to the Mayans. The calendar, in addition to tracking and predicting cycles, also predicted the exact day that the Spaniards would arrive on the shores of Central America.

Cortez arrived in Mexico in 1519. These events were recorded in the Dresden codex, which is one of the few texts to survive to this day aside from the oral tradition of the Jaguar priests. These sources predict events leading up to 2012, such as the thrones of power being turned upside down, fire, bloodshed, and violence leading up to a cosmic calamity and deluge.

By 2008 we can expect very dramatic weather changes, which include the slowing down of the Gulf Stream, a dramatic rise of the world's oceans, and increased earthquake and volcanic activity. This evolutionary shift requires preparation on a spiritual level, rather than just a physical one.

MAYAN ASTROLOGY

Each of us has our own Mayan name and affirmation, which is calculated by birthdates and numerology. I have researched names for many people, and every time their galactic signature is determined, it's always a perfect match for who they really are at heart.

In addition there are 13 galactic tones and twenty solar seals which go further to incorporate our service, empowerment and lifestyle into a more naturally harmonious flow with the days and weeks of the calendar.

I have researched the astrology seals and the corresponding birth signs for myself, and my Mayan calendar name, or "galactic signature," is Red Solar Dragon.

The significance of the dragon represents the very first of the twenty solar seals of the twenty solar tribes. The dragon initiates birth and the state of being. The affirmation of this name is:

"I pulse in order to nurture... realizing being with the solar tone of intention, I am guided by the power of navigation...which is the power of synchronicity."

Each 7-day week cycle has a corresponding charka assigned to it:

The first day is the crown charka,
the 2nd is the root charka,
the 3rd is the 3rd eye charka,
the 4th is the sacral charka,
the 5th is the throat charka,
the 6th is the solar plexus charka,
and the 7th is the heart charka.

Each of the 13 months has a corresponding affirmation:

Moon 1	July 26 – August 21	Moon of Purpose
Moon 2	August 22 – September 19	Moon of Challenge
Moon 3	September 20 – October 18	Moon of Service
Moon 4	October 19 – November 14	Moon of Form
Moon 5	November 15 – December 12	Moon of Radiance
Moon 6	December 13 – January 9	Moon of Equality
Moon 7	January 10 – February 6	Moon of Attunement
Moon 8	February 7 – March 6	Moon of Integrity
Moon 9	March 7 – April 3	Moon of Intention
Moon 10	April 4 – May 1	Moon of Manifestation
Moon 11	May 2 – May 30	Moon of Liberation
Moon 12	May 31 – June 26	Moon of Cooperation
Moon 13	June 27 – July 24	Moon of Presence

Knowing which day is influenced by which charka and the month's overall intention can provide powerful insight and benefit in planning and predicting our immediate future.

Imagine the overwhelming unifying effect that this form of time keeping would have if it were adopted by the entire world.

The possibilities would be unlimited.

The return to astrological awareness in our day-to-day lives binds us with the movements and rhythms of cosmic forces that imprint upon us at birth and guides us through the cycles of our life.

Until we can create this new paradigm on a global scale, we can initiate this for ourselves, which is a great place to start.

UFOs Crop Circles The Mayan Calendar and Sacred Places

Crop Circles
The Message
And The Mechanics

© Rob Simone

B eautiful as they are mysterious, the world's center of crop circle activity is only a few hours outside of the bustling city of London.

I lived in London for over a year and made countless visits to the countryside where these stunning formations have been reported as far back as the 1600's.

Rob Simone

Researching these complex symbols has taken me on many journeys around the world exploring the physical and metaphysical aspects of this phenomenon.

CROP CIRCLES: THE EVIDENCE

On one particular research expedition, I set out for Avebury, which is just a few hours drive from London and is home to Stonehenge and other megalithic sites. I was equipped with a range of detection equipment including dowsing rods, electromagnetic field detectors, and a Geiger counter.

At the crack of dawn, I set up an observation post atop a hill and scanned the area with high-powered binoculars and thermal imaging cameras. I spotted an elliptical formation a few miles away. I packed up the gear and followed the unpaved access roads to the edge of the field.

Walking up to this newly formed crop formation near Silbury Hill, the largest man made mound in Europe, I began taking readings and discovered an elevated level of gamma radiation.

I scanned the area around the field, and found no other "hot spots" other than the formation. There were also deformities in the affected wheat stalk, which seem to confirm my feeling that this was not a "man made" formation.

Far too often crop circles are the product of hoaxers or the local druid population who sometimes use crop formations for rituals and ceremonies.

When it comes to crop circles, the scientific approach requires something to be measured. Biophysical experiments on the affected wheat within crop circles have yielded reproducible results. These findings included variances in growth rates between "circle wheat" and unaffected wheat. The seeds taken out of the seed heads of wheat within crop circles have a completely different germination behavior than the seeds taken from wheat outside of formations in the standing crop.

There are also atomic variances within the cells of the plants, which are easily seen through a microscope. This cellular change is accompanied by a chemical change, which is probably why the circle wheat seeds germinate differently in comparison to normal seeds.

The seeds from crop circles have been observed to grow three to four times faster than seeds from normal crops.

You can simulate some effects that are found in crop circles with the use of microwave radiation. Indeed, many eyewitnesses have reported an increased heat signature to recently created crop circles. Some have described this heat as boiling hot, and burn marks have also been found near formations. Dramatic changes to the chemical composition of the soil have also been recorded.

I have noticed in many formations that the soil appears to be very dry in an otherwise muddy field. Another unusual feature of crop circles are their shape when they are formed on slopes or hillsides. The crop circles become elliptic, and the long axis of the ellipse falls in line with the slope of the hill, or with the maximum gradient. Flattening crops with a board and a rope cannot reproduce these various anomalies. Even with the current level of technology that the military possesses, it would seem that it would not fully explain all of the components that some crop circles possess.

Rob Simone

Floating balls of light are often seen in conjunction with the formation of crop circles, many of which have even been captured on videotape. Some of these sightings also show military helicopters in pursuit of this aerial phenomenon. I have seen videos showing a light floating over a field in Avebury, which splits in two, and is soon followed by a black Apache-style attack helicopter. The helicopter follows the balls of light for several minutes at which point the balls join together and continue at the same velocity.

The British government has a long history in investigating UFOs and crop circles, and their aircraft are often photographed in the same frame as these phenomena.

Many times a very strong magnetic field is left behind, and is enough to affect a hand held compass. Very often people with cameras and video recorders notice an instant drain of their batteries once they enter some crop circles.

While I was looking at some of the photographs from my past fieldwork, I came across a curious pattern that I hadn't noticed before.

In the close ups of the wheat that had been laid down, there was small blades of grass amongst them that seemed to be completely unaffected.

I found again and again examples of grass popping up through the flattened crop. This seemed strange because wheat is a very stiff and hearty plant. It takes a bit of force to compress it, especially when there is such a dense grouping of it as there is in the crop fields.

How could a blade of grass, as thin as it is, withstand the forces strong enough to bend the crops to the ground?

© Rob Simone

© Rob Simone

This observation lead me to the conclusion that whatever force is at work to make these patterns is "frequency specific" to the plant for which it's intended. This force could be exactly "tuned" to resonate with the molecular pattern of the wheat and nothing else. This careful calibration further suggests a highly intelligent consciousness behind this phenomenon.

Rob Simone

CROP CIRCLES: THE EXPERIENCE

Of the hundreds of crop patterns I've encountered in different places around the world, no two are the same in shape or *sensation*.

One particular incident left me with a new understanding that only comes from exploring the phenomenon meta-physically rather than just scientifically.

Near Tilshead, 10 miles north west of Stonehenge, I happened upon a newly formed crop formation just as the sun was coming up. I began taking readings and discovered an unusually strong DC magnetic field. Being inside the circle itself left me with a feeling of dizziness and light-headedness like I had never known before.

It was as if gravity was tugging on me from every direction, and whether I moved my hand up, down, left, or right, it was as though gravity was pulling in the opposite direction. I felt a need to lie down and shield my eyes from the sun. The air was damp and thick from the soaking dew that covered the ground. The wheat was warm and pungent and I could taste it with each breath.

The more I gasped, the harder it was to get any air. It was then I felt myself falling through a black void as if the ground had suddenly given way beneath me. The feeling of dizziness was replaced by a clear sensation of falling and then weightlessness.

UFOs Crop Circles The Mayan Calendar and Sacred Places

© Rob Simone

No longer able to feel my body, I began to navigate through this strange dimension. As in lucid dreams, I directed my thoughts towards the stars and attempted to move out into space.

As I was doing that I realized I was not alone and was in the company of many other beings observing me. At that instant I was engaged in direct mental telepathic communication at a rate so fast, it moved at the speed of thought.

As soon as a question was formed in my mind, the answer was immediately given by one or several different entities. Their questions were asked and answered by me at the same speed. From this exchange I asked the usual questions about the nature of their existence and the place I was now in.

Then quickly it moved on to a general lesson to the nature of the universe and the different levels of reality beyond the physical plane.

The crop circle phenomenon was part of that experience insofar as it was a gateway or portal to this dimensional plane, and to the entities that created it.

During this instantaneous communication it was revealed that some crop circles are for many people and some are for just a few. Crop circles are the intersection between the standard form of energy displacement utilized by these beings and the crop itself, who do so deliberately, with the intent of expressing healing messages through mathematical and geometric concepts.

These symbols are the foundation on which these beings understand and process information. Their use of words only arises when in telepathic communication with humans, and then, it is only possible when the human has been conditioned on a conscious or subconscious level to understand them.

This conditioning is like a computer program that is downloaded into the person's memory. It is a series of symbols that are connected to specific areas of the brain that control speech and comprehension.

The person could be unaware that these symbols have been downloaded in them. Only when these entities initiate contact, do they activate the matrix of symbols already inside the mind that corresponds to the language center of the brain, thereby allowing instantaneous communication. It is not uncommon for someone who has gone through this process to recognize shapes and patterns in crop circles and in other natural phenomena that are completely invisible to other people.

The entities conveyed a sense of their "local community" that had been connected with that part of England for centuries and had just as many questions about us as we would have for them. The construction of the crop patterns represent a small avenue of access they have to interact and communicate with our physical dimension.

I heard a strange humming noise, felt completely dizzy, and decided to leave the circle. It was then I noticed the farmer whose land I was on, approaching from the service road. His name was O'Boyle, and he was coming to investigate this newly formed crop circle.

He told me it wasn't there yesterday and must have appeared overnight. I asked him if this was the first time he had had these glyphs appear on his land.

He told me of a formation he found a few years prior that was rather small and on a remote part of his farm. When he noticed it, he walked up to the crop to take a closer look and noticed that there were no footprints or paths leading in or out of the circle from the surrounding wheat.

He did not go into the circle himself, but rather looked at it to attempt an explanation. Just then a flock of migrating birds were coming over the hill directly in front of him.

Flying in the usual V formation, there were at least twenty of them flying close enough that he could see that they were going to pass exactly over his location.

Just as the birds were directly overhead something amazing happened. They parted, some to the left, the others to the right, and none of them flew over the top of the crop circle, which lied directly in their path. As they flew around the formation, he turned around to see that they once again came back together to form the typical V formation, and stayed that way until they were out of sight.

Birds are extremely sensitive to magnetic fields, and they use the earth's magnetic field to navigate over great distances. It might also be possible that they are able to "detect" the lay lines and variances in the earth's fields to find their way over thousands of miles during migration.

85

As the farmer left I turned my attention back to the crop circle. I thought it might be a good idea to take some measurements with my dowsing rods to see if there were any energy fields that could be detected.

THE ANCIENT TOOL OF DOWSING

Dowsing rods have been used for thousands of years to find water and lost items.

Dowsers are often used to find the location where ranchers should drill to find water. They are still used today with great accuracy. In the days of old a dowsing rod was made of wood and consisted of a tree branch with two ends connected in the middle. A dowser would walk over the ground. When the stick pointed downwards, that's where the location was.

Studying ancient cultures and comparative religion throughout my life, I often thought of Moses traveling through the desert with his staff and the Israelites. It occurred to me that the many accounts of Moses finding water during the exodus in the dessert by using his staff to find springs of water, was actually an ancient account of a dowsing rod.

Exodus 17

"God told Moses, "Walk on ahead of the people and take with you some elders of Israel …and in hand the rod with which you struck the Nile."

" Behold, I will stand before thee there upon the rock in Horeb; and thou shalt smite the rock, and there shall come water out of it, that the people may drink"

Many dowsing rods today are made of copper and silver and are able to freely rotate on an axis.

I used this type inside the crop circle.

When I began to use them, I noticed that there was no wind, and started to slowly make my way toward the center of the formation. Soon the rods began to shift back and forth, and as I approached the center, their movements became more erratic. Near the center, they were in a state of nonstop flux, which confirmed to me the presence of extraordinary energy field.

I made my way out of the formation and back to the Barge Inn Pub.

© Rob Simone

The Barge Inn is a meeting place for all crop circle explorers. In the back poolroom, there are large maps on the walls with thumbtacks showing each location of the crop circles.

I started to drink pints of cider and the bartender began to tell me about his pub and the people that come there. He said that there was a lay line that ran right through the center of the bar, and funny enough, the local farmers seemed to be able to sense it!

The men would come in and sit on one side, and the women on the other. As I finished off my third pint of cider, I ordered a Guinness Stout and realized it would take some time to fill. I began to casually look around and saw that in fact the men were all to the left of the invisible lay line and the women were all on the right.

I talked with the pub owner all night until he locked the doors and we were left inside with a few others to continue our "research." It was a hell of a night. Never before have I heard so many stories about crop circles from the people who actually plant the crop.

The farmers had a unique perspective and they spoke of the many generations before them who also saw strange things in the fields but rarely spoke of them. Some of these stories involved the sons and daughters of the farmers who would disappear for days only to be found later in the fields next to or in a crop circle unable to explain how they got there.

Other farmers spoke of lights in the sky and unexplainable communications with mysterious entities who would tell them about the "life force" plants have and even the best time to plant and harvest them!

It's ironic that the people with the most knowledge are often the ones who speak the least. Talking with the farmers made me realize the importance crop circles may hold for humanity and the future of the planet, but also for individuals who actually step into them and the larger universe they represent

UFOs – Past, Present and Future

The abundance of ancient references to "Star people," gods in "flying chariots" and advanced technology written into hundreds of historical accounts, woven into oral traditions and depicted in folk art dating back as far as 30,000 years lays the foundation of the UFO/E.T. contact in many past civilizations.

The explosion of reports, video documentation, eyewitness accounts, and official sourced testimony over the last 30 years demonstrates a clear and continual rise in the frequency of contact cases and sightings now being documented.

With this, comes an unprecedented level of "official" disclosure events like the release of the Mexican Air Force footage, the testimony of the Russian Air Force generals, and the Brazilian government's formal recognition of the field of Ufology. The latest opinion polls reflect the public's growing interest and belief that some UFO's represent intelligent contact from beyond our world.

All of these factors clearly point to an expansion of the field of Ufology and the inevitable impact it will have on politics, religion, technology and society.

Rob Simone

Ufology, in my opinion, should be seen as an "emerging science" to reflect the deeply held belief of humanity's place in a larger universe.

No longer isolated by time and space, no longer kept hidden by secretive governments, the truth of the on-going human interaction with other races from beyond the stars will expand and unite the awareness of the collective consciousness and diminish the destructive and limiting characteristics of earthly belief systems.

You get to reach these conclusions, in my case, by poring over the thousands of eyewitness reports and examining the thousands of declassified government documents that prove beyond a shadow of a doubt that this phenomenon is taking place, not only in the skies above, but directly to us.

There are vast amounts of theories to try to explain the constant involvement of extra-terrestrial contacts that have been reported by people from every walk of life, and from every quarter of the globe.

There is an abundance of evidence that suggests some sort of off world or extra-dimensional intelligence was in touch with the great civilizations of Sumer, Egypt and other ancient cultures. There are many examples in cave paintings dating back 20,000 years and medieval and renaissance artwork that show clear UFO type objects and humanoids that don't conform to the natural environment or experience of the artists of that time.

Recently, in our modern militarized world, ufologists have drawn many conclusions about the frequency of UFO reports in relation to nuclear missiles and advanced military activity.

I have traveled around the world, through 27 different countries researching the E.T. phenomenon from the Asian, Middle Eastern,

Aboriginal, and European perspectives, only to find it is just as prevalent in their societies as it is in the West.

From as far back as man was able to scratch out an image on a cave wall, to today, with newspapers and global news agencies, UFOs have been recorded, researched and reported on as part of the yet un-disclosed component of human history.

The Spirituality of Disclosure

A look into the larger universe or the landscape of our mind can be a journey we take for a moment or a lifetime. Sometimes we are plunged into a larger perspective by sudden events.

Sometimes we see through the cracks of our reality into another one like the flickering flame of a distant candle.

There are many reasons for our individual search for a greater understanding of our own "true nature" and the workings of the universe. Our connection to the source of creation has both a personal and communal aspect to it.

To find a lifestyle that balances both aspects in harmony is the goal of many searching souls.

The Spirituality of Disclosure is a tug on our consciousness, a question: Do you want to go on as you have or are you ready to let go and turn a corner in you life?

Be mindful of your thoughts, for they become your words…
Notice how your words become your actions…
Reflect on how your actions become your character…
Your character becomes your destiny.

The single most important lesson for people in this world to learn is their place in the larger universe and within their own thoughts.

Until we do so, we will continue to be burdened with the global conflicts of religion, country, power and greed.

In fact, it is this distraction, these wars, these petty differences that serve to keep us from understanding this larger reality.

It's this bickering and fighting amongst our own ranks, the human ranks, that keeps us occupied and distracted from simply looking up and understanding our place in the larger universe.

For those not engaged in war or global conquest, the distraction comes in many other forms, and these forms of distractions, are easy to recognize.

Whatever pulls your attention from a larger perspective, a global mentality, open awareness, an understanding of the whole scope of your place in the grand spectrum of life in the universe.

Whatever pulls you from that high position to getting you focus down to things that just get you caught up, and we lose your place, you lose your sense of this bird's eye view, and you fall in the mire of the creeping malaise of distraction.

When you're in this malaise, by the way, it's not a terrible place to be; that's why so many people are in it, and can stay in it for so long. It's filled with a lot of the things we like; we take comfort in this area of consciousness.

How do we take comfort from this realm of distraction?

There are a lot of things that exist among these realms, like inflated emotions.

Our culture validates envy, the foolish guffaw and lusting after things.

This level of distraction creates an environment that allows rash judgment and petty behavior because it is the space we get into when we are rushed, self-absorbed and caught up in our dramas and the influence of our overactive mind.

We sometime confuse childishness with youthful spirit.

We like being immature; in fact, we have raised the bar on acceptability on immaturity in a pervasive way in our culture.

Overindulgence is also down on this level, eating all the wrong things all the time or spending money frivolously or excess television and entanglements with family or relationships.

The mind has back ups: it has forgetfulness, it has projection, it has denial, it has all sorts ways in which we can act out to handle the difficulties in life in a way that is automatic and ingrained in our behavioral responses. This method of dealing with things becomes our personality, and can be difficult to examine, and even harder to consider revising.

It's like we are a factory, we process information but when you put something in that cogs the system, that doesn't fit, it has a way of dealing with it, down the well-traveled drain in a un-processed form, without the opportunity to *learn* from the experience.

We didn't know how to deal with the experience so we hit the automatic garbage chute.

Any time that happens to you, it should send off a warning bell. Any time you don't know how to deal with a situation, you *should* know how to deal with it even if you *don't know* how to deal with it.

Meaning, that you don't need to know the answers to everything, you don't even need to know what to say when you are in that situation.

That is when you're called to be a "fully operational" human being, because a fully operational human is someone who is able to deal with any situation.

There is a knowing, an intuition, in all of us, but when we give up our connection to it, we have to rely on our often failed way of dealing with things. The connection is best when we are calm and centered.

Self doubt and the realm of distraction is the ever-calling "siren song" that leads us to our doom.

When we are centered, we are tapping into part of our brain that is the psychic part, that's the intuitive part. It's the part that taps into this higher consciousness, the global awareness, the remote viewing, this shamanistic way of dealing with this stuff, this part of the brain is what a fully operational human knows how to tap into.

When you are operating from a higher consciousness and an intuitive state, you are off the hook. You don't have to worry about doing the right thing or doing the wrong thing, all of that evaporates instantly.

When you are operating from your center, the right words come, the right response come, the right actions come, because you are not listening to the nervous chattering voices in your head, whose dialogue are written by the ego. You are listening to a pure, higher intuitive source.

How does one maintain sitting on a high perch, in a sense, to be in this intuitive, higher conscious state?

It simply means you're not in the level of distraction, you're not in that lower level, you can still deal with it, and understand it, and appreciate and deal with people who are in that mode, but you just don't have to go down there to do it.

That's why toilet plungers have handles.

Now how does this fit in with the ET stuff?

The most important lesson that we humans have to learn is our place in a larger universe.

From that stems the life lessons we need to understand our place in the world.

It is the equivalent to one person understanding his or her own place in life.

So many years from now, humans in a new age who are space faring, and in touch with other E.T.s, would be of the mindset....

...we know we are here on earth but there is a whole galaxy out there that we're aware of....

...our actions, speech, intent, and thought corresponds to that,

so each person has mindset of global awareness.

To be in the realm of higher consciousness intuitive state, at peace, and operating from your center, requires you to say, think, and do things that reflect this awareness. When you are thinking and saying and doing and being this awareness, that's when you're in the state of not having to worry about saying the wrong thing.

That's the bridge to getting more of us over to operating in a higher state, which is the bridge, ultimately, for the people of this planet to be operating at, to move the planetary awareness to a point that could make us ready to expand our relationship to races and intelligences outside our world.

Beware!

Operating from this higher center of consciousness, where the perils of right and wrong and how to act are alleviated, comes with a price.

You can't unlearn something.

You may miss the company in the realms of distraction; after all, you did spend a lot of time there, and there are a lot of people still there…

You may feel a little different; even your friends may notice this.

Some people don't like to be different; they prefer to

"go along … to get along."

When you receive knowledge that challenges, undermines, threatens, or even destroys a part of your tightly-held belief system, that's when you start to cling to them even tighter.

What most people cling to are, the major belief systems that dominate this planet. Islam, Judaism and Christianity.

The rapid rate of technology and ever-increasing evidence of extra-solar life will push many religious followers into a difficult reality to face, one that the holy texts and the "leaders of faith" may not adequately answer. It is then that we need to take our existing faith and set it against a **larger backdrop**, not abandon it all at once. The "hows" and "whys" of that is a subject on which I will speak about often and in my next book "Beyond All Borders."

Don't let your beliefs blind you or detour you from new information.

**Genuine ignorance is... profitable because it is likely to be accompanied by humility, curiosity, and open mindedness; whereas, the ability to repeat catch-phrases, recant terms, familiar propositions, gives the conceit of knowledge and coats the mind with a varnish waterproof to new ideas.
~John Dewey**

Feel as though you are already at this level, and want to be in contact with other realms?

You can open up a window to the universe in front of you whenever you like. All it takes is belief, understanding and intention.

The underlying message is that if we want planetary E.T. contact, we have to adopt this mindset for a global * "100th monkey" awareness.

We have to click this big switch, this big lever for the planetary field of mind to say aah… we understand our place in the galaxy we are not alone.

That is the first step.

That planetary "switch" has to be thrown and when it does, it's going to ease tensions and perhaps allow increased public and personal extra-terrestrial and extra dimensional contact to begin.

Suffering and negativity will be lessened.

For the 100th monkey switch to be thrown, it will take mass acceptance of the E.T. reality. The long-standing cover up of the reality of E.T. life by the powers that be, constitutes a dramatic evolutional setback for all mankind and is truly a crime against humanity.

For those of us who have taken in this E.T. reality, we are no longer able to go back to that "play" we once were in. It's now the characters in the play that are rewriting the story as they see fit.

The characters realize they are the actors, and have a choice of what they say, do, and what the ending will be of whatever play they find themselves in.

It's time to take down the set. The play that still has so many people playing in it, some knowingly others unknowing, is telling a story of our planet all alone in a vast universe.

Keep the actors, but change the script.

This change is not going to happen from the outside in,

it's going to happen from the inside out.

So, little did some of you know, the whole field of Ufology is really about something inside of **you**.

It's really about how you think and how you engage the world.

And I'm telling you it's changeable.

It begins with your thoughts:

If you're negatively and awkwardly thinking,

you're negatively and awkwardly acting.

Operating out of a larger perspective, when you maintain it, will deflect the things that pull you off your center and cloud your judgment.

Now remember the price…

It means also taking full responsibility for our actions; no longer will the trite, immature or cruel things get swept under the carpet.

Zen Quote:
Infinite gratitude for all things past
Infinite compassion for all things present
Infinite responsibility for all things future

Knowing your place in your own life, and also your place in the world, is equivalent to the world knowing its place in the galaxy.

The same thing as the cells in our body, they must operate as their individual functions, but also in the operation of the larger organism.

If one cell told another cell, "there really is no larger organism we're part of, it's just us here," the cell would have wrong information, it would operate abnormally, and the organism would suffer.

We humans are perhaps like cells, the earth is the being.

The earth is a cell, and our galaxy is the being.

Our galaxy is a cell, the universe is the being.

Perhaps the universe is a cell, within a larger being we don't yet have a name for.

When our planet operates as a "being" it can engage the galaxy as such.

Rob Simone

We should never lose sight of the fact that there is more going on to us and around us that what we can perceive with our five senses. Our five-sense reality is not the limit of all that there is.

When you realize and believe that you're not alone in the universe, you open yourself up to all these miracles that can happen, such as healings, psychic abilities, and all the phenomena that's associated with extra dimensional beings. It releases your potential and instills a knowing that you operate on these levels, too.

* In 1952, on the island of Koshima, Japan, scientists fed monkeys with sweet potatoes.

One monkey learned to wash the potatoes with water and taught this trick to her mother. Soon others learned as well.

In the autumn of 1958, a breakthrough occurred when monkeys on other islands and the mainland at Takasakiyama also began washing their sweet potatoes.

Awareness is contagious to *everyone*, when there is enough of it.

UFOs Crop Circles The Mayan Calendar and Sacred Places

The Gods of Babylon
The Societies of the Occult

© Rob Simone

Most knowledgeable historians and Freemasons claim that Nimrod, builder of the Tower of Babel, was the father of what was to develop into modern-day Freemasonry.

In studying ancient religions, it appears that there are many gods. I will attempt to unravel a little-known truth: that the ancients worshipped only a handful of gods that once were their post flood forefathers. The existence of, and allusion to, many gods in pagan religions could be explained by examining a famous story in the bible.

(1) In the Old Testament, when ancient patriarchs were scattered abroad following the confusion of tongues at Babylon, their names were changed and altered in the many new languages, and

(2) Ancestor worship transmuted these patriarchs into gods. Hence, what appears to be the worship of multiple gods could actually be the worship of Noah, Shem, Ham, and his descendants (with the exclusion of Japheth) under many names in all pagan nations.

Cush, for example, the son of Ham, and his family migrated to Africa with Ham following the confusion of tongues in Babylon. As a result of the confusion of tongues, many new languages spread throughout the known world. Thus, Cush was manifested in as many names. In Babylon, Cush was known as Bel.

We know this by tracing Nimrod, son of Cush. In ancient Assyria, Ninus is said to be the founder of Nineveh. Nineveh means "the habitation of Ninus." The name of the chief part of the ruins of Nineveh is Nimrod. Ninus couls actually be Nimrod, who in scripture is the son of Cush. Ninus is also said to have been the son of Bel, co-founder of Ba-bel. Thus Cush more than likely is Bel.

In the Chronicles of Eusebius, Ninus is listed as the first Assyrian king. Assyria listed kings from the first Babylonian kings, since Nineveh was founded from Babylon. Further, in other Babylonian inscriptions, it states that Bel, or Belus, the father of Ninus, founded Babylon.

There seem to be no contradiction here. In established eastern mythology, Cush was an instigator of the "great apostasy" at Babel. Cush may have been the founder of the new Babylonian religion, but Nimrod, was the architect and builder of that religion, and the first king of Babylon. It is also understood that if the son was identified with the father, it is fitting that the name "Bel" descend to the son by inheritance and lineage of family.

In researching this concept, I found a trail of evidence from the deification of Cush following his death, and his translation into a sun-god in many lands and languages. In Phoenicia, Cush was Chush, the sun-god, worshiped by all and the first person of the Phoenician Trinity.

In the Greek language, the god Hermes, who also is identified very closely with the sun, is a synonym for the "son of Ham," or Cush. Hermes was known as the great original prophet of idolatry and was recognized by the pagans as the author of their religious rites, something that, in my opinion, further identifies him with Cush. Hermes was also known as the interpreter and scribe of the gods, meaning he understood their mysteries.

© Rob Simone

It is here that we can first connect Cush with Freemasonry, for Masons claim Hermes as one of their more important religious patriarchs. Mackey's Encyclopedia of Freemasonry states, "In all the old manuscript records which contain the legend of the Craft, mention is made of Hermes as one of the founders of Freemasonry."

Hermes was also claimed by the Alchemists to be the founder of their art, which became known as Hermetic Science. The Rosicrucians, who developed the hermetic rites and hermetic degrees in France during the last half of the eighteenth century, took up the study of this art. According to Mackey, this group was commonly known as the Illuminati.

Most important to this study will be Cush's Chaldean name, "Chaos," for this descriptive name and the career Cush followed have both been identified with the conspiratorial 33rd degree Supreme Council of Freemasonry. Their "Great Work" is to bring "order out of chaos" through world government. The Latin words "ORDO AB CHAO" are inscribed on the 33rd degree jewel presented to the advanced Mason and is one of the mottos of the institution.

Also, Nimrod, son of Cush, is the father of the Babylonian religion and all its progeny of polytheistic, idolatrous religion. Nimrod's ancient mystery school, which is the mother of all harlot religions, expounded in Revelations 17, 18 which could imply the modern Mystery Babylon school's war against God for control of men's souls.

Today some Freemasons continue to obligate themselves to Nimrod through blood oaths, for this "mighty one" is considered the founder of Freemasonry. In the New Encyclopedia of Freemasonry, 32nd degree English Freemason, A. E. Waite, confirms that Nimrod, "as founder of the Babylonian monarchy . . . was Grand Master of all masons and a builder of many cities in Shinar "It is Babylon which figures in the annals of this kind of Masonic belief . . ."

UFOs Crop Circles The Mayan Calendar and Sacred Places

© Rob Simone

Belus, Bel and Baal, are all the same sun-god representing Cush, the father of Nimrod. Nimrod is also known as Bel, for in eastern mythology, the son is always identified with his father.

Therefore, upon the death of Cush, Nimrod inherited the title of Bel.

Bel or Baal worship was curtailed following the death of Nimrod, who was judicially put to death to send a message to pagan priests throughout the world to abolish his religion, or face the same fate. The supreme judges who sentenced him also decreed that all record of his exploits be obliterated, forbidding even the utterance of his name.

Hence, over the generations, Nimrod became insignificant and even unknown to the masses of men—but not to the adepts in Mystery Babylon. Nimrod's priesthood literally went underground with their religion.

To avoid exposure, the ancient Babylonian priesthood met in caverns beneath the earth and there developed an elaborate system of secret rituals that would take the initiate priest by degrees through a hodgepodge of deities—all of whom represented Nimrod in his various manifestations—in a search for his original "lost name." In the final initiation the ancient priesthood would whisper Nimrod's Babylonian name "Bel" in the ear of the initiated priest, who was then told to never divulge this secret "lost name" of God.

In building the Tower of Babel, Nimrod (under the name of Belus), is said to have separated heaven and earth from one another and formed the "new order of things." Nimrod's tower was built to war against Almighty God to keep Him from interfering with the lives of those on earth. As such, Nimrod is represented as the reformer of the world or founder of a New World Order, or New Secular Order. God saw his wickedness and destroyed his efforts.

In our day, Freemasonry has taken up Nimrod's unfinished work of the Tower of Babel, symbolized by the unfinished pyramid on the back of the U.S. $1 bill. Surrounding the pyramid are Latin words, which translated mean "Announcing the birth of a New Secular Order," or "New World Order" which has fallen into popular theories of a grand, global covert agenda, which may or may not have some truth in it.

The significance of this symbol in relationship to Freemasonry's founding of the United States of America for a particular and peculiar reason should be explored.

It has emerged in my research that the pagan doctrine of male and female gods was conceived in the mind of the wife of Nimrod. While Nimrod was considered by the pagans to be the father of the gods, his wife, Semiramis, was the mother of the gods. Although Semiramis is not mentioned in Scripture, she is mentioned in Assyrian history as the wife of Ninus. Ninus, you recall, was Nimrod.

Following the confusion of tongues, as told in the Old Testament, when the inhabitants of Babylon were scattered abroad, Nimrod and Semiramis became known by a myriad of names in as many languages. Semiramis, the actual author of the pagan fertility rites, is said to have survived her husband by forty-two years.

D. Mellis

During this time she developed the worship of mother and child, which, according to Alexander Hislop, is reflected in the multiple mother-child deities of pagan religions.

"In Egypt, the Mother and the Child were worshipped under the names of Isis and Osiris. In India, even to this day, as Isi and Iswara; in Asia, as Cybele and Deoius; in pagan Rome as Fortuna and Jupiter-puer, or Jupiter, the boy; in Greece, as Ceres the Great Mother, with the babe at her breast, or as Irene, the goddess of Peace, with the boy Plutos in her arms. . . The winged boy-god Cupid, the son of Venus. . . Feronia, the goddess of Liberty and her youthful son Jupiter."

Most of the mother goddesses can be traced back to Semiramis, who was a "paragon of unbridled lust and licentiousness," writes Hislop. She impressed upon the minds of those postdiluvian inhabitants of the world her depraved and polluted character.

Semiramis was worshipped as the benignant virgin, Rhea, the great Mother of the gods, but with atrocious rites that identified her with Venus, the goddess and Mother of all impurity. From Venus we receive our English word "venereal."

How to explain the paradox found in mystery religions of a goddess of lust assuming the character and attributes of a revered mother? Is this a loose interpretation of the historical record, or a byproduct of human religious design?

Hislop examines several pagan myths that teach that the mother goddess was both wife and mother of the father of the gods, and explains how this doctrine evolved.

He suggests that the promiscuous Semiramis became pregnant following the death of Nimrod. To alleviate embarrassment, she proclaimed herself a virgin impregnated by a ray of light shot from the sun. In her womb was the promised seed of redemption. When the illegitimate male child was born, she taught the people that he was Nimrod reincarnated. Thus, we find in paganism the Mother goddess presented first as wife, then as mother of the same person.

Semiramis allotted to her illegitimate son all the attributes of the savior of mankind, and presented herself as the "woman who bore the Savior," thus guaranteeing her own deification. Hislop says "in life her husband had been honored as a hero; in death she will have him worshiped as a god, yea, as the woman's promised seed, 'Zero-Ashta,' who was destined to bruise the serpent's head, and who, in doing so, was to have his own heel bruised."

In the course of time, both Semiramis and her son Nimrod, as Mother goddess and Son were worshipped with enthusiasm that was incredible, and their images were everywhere and adored.

It has been demonstrated that Semiramis following the death of Nimrod developed the sex religion of Babylon. The history of its development and propagation is preserved in the legend of Osiris and Isis of Egypt.

Osiris was the Egyptian name for Nimrod, and Isis was the Egyptian name given to Semiramis.

It seems clear that pagan symbols have subtly infiltrated Christian holy days, we need only look at Easter, a celebrated date of the resurrection of Jesus Christ.

What most Christians do not know is that Easter is one of the names given to Semiramis. This name is traced back to the pagan goddess Astarte, which we have learned is Semiramis. British Archaeologist Austen Layard (1817-1894) discovered Astarte was also given the name Ishtar. In the spring of each year, Ishtar the fertility goddess, was commemorated by decorating the Ishtar egg, a symbol of impregnation, or fertility. From Ishtar comes our English word "Easter."

During the Master Mason (3rd Degree) initiation, much emphasis is placed on the reenactment of the death, burial, and resurrection of a personality named Hiram Abiff.

That the ritual represents the myth of Osiris makes the pagan ancestry of Freemasonry clear; for Osiris is simply another manifestation of the Babylonian father of gods, Nimrod.

The Masonic legend of Hiram Abiff is constructed around the builder of Solomon's Temple, Hiram of Tyre the widow's son (1 Kings 7:13-14). In the Masonic version of this legend, Hiram Abiff held in confidence the secret of the Master Mason, called the "Master's Word" or the "lost name of God." Three ruffians named Jubela, Jubelo, and Jubelum demand the last name from its possessor, Hiram Abiff.

After refusing to divulge it, Hiram was killed, entombed for 14 days, then raised from the dead by Solomon, who is played by the Worshipful Master of the Lodge.

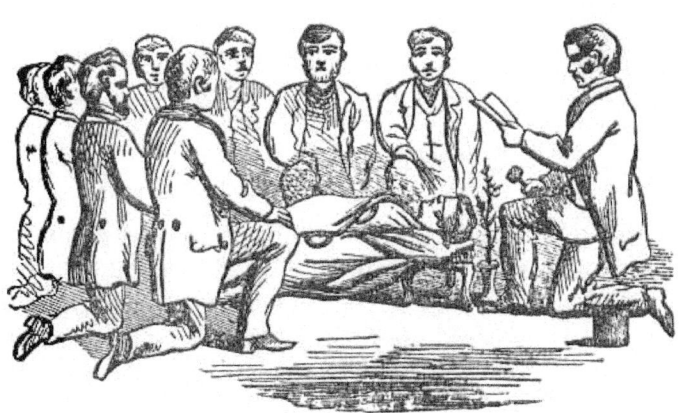

Funeral of Hiram Abiff

(The name Sol-om-on, could be the composite name of the three sun-gods in Roman, Indian, and Egyptian mythology.) Solomon then whispers the lost name "Jebulon" in the initiate's ear, which when broken down into its three component parts is Jah-Bel-On, the sun-gods of Syria, Babylon, and Egypt, all of whom represented Nimrod.

The basic similarity between the Hiram Abiff and Osiris legends concerns the generative power. As we know, in the legend of the death of Osiris, what could not be recovered was the penis, or generative power of the deceased god. Likewise, confirms Freemason Wagner, "the lost word . . . is but the lost generative power of the architect of the temple, Hiram Abiff." This understanding of the Hiram Abiff story is supported by the Masonic interpretation of the Square and Compass, which symbolically equates Masonic "architecture" with sexual intercourse and spiritual and creative powers.

To illustrate the sun-god's method of building the universe, the Babylonians adorned the walls of their temples either with carvings of men and women in actual intercourse with their bodies positioned as if they were carpenter tools, or with mosaics of carpenter tools arranged geometrically to portray the same act of sexual intercourse. Over time these phallic symbols became objects of adoration. Worship of the phallus (or reproductive organs) is today euphemistically described as fertility worship.

Some Babylonian priesthoods taught that good works were acquired by worshipping their creator-god through licentious temple ceremonies.

Eastern kings were expected to patronize, protect, and propagate these manufactured religions, which were presided over by a powerful priesthood. And since Mystery Babylon's priests were self-ordained "wise men," kings inevitably selected their advisors from among them.

Royal Courts were thus full of magicians, astrologers, soothsayers, and Chaldeans. The Chaldean race was especially familiar with the wisdom of the ancients.

It was in ancient Babylon that the union between religion and state began. Although kings ruled, pagan priests were the covert power behind their thrones. We shall refer to this arrangement as "the Babylonia System," for it is this union of religion and state that identifies the headquarters of modern Mystery Babylon.

Meanwhile, the priests of ancient Mystery Babylon had one goal in mind: the control of the populace through a monopoly of politics and religion. If an ancient king became too demanding, decided to change religions, or threatened the priestly caste, his reign was cut short by a conspiracy of the priesthood.

Such a conspiracy followed the death of Nebuchadnezzar in 562 B.C. In less than six years, murder passed the scepter to three of the king's descendants. Finally Nabonidus ascended the Babylonia throne in 556 B.C.

Nabonidus entered the ranks of nobility by marrying one of Nebuchadnezzar's daughters. Two years before his ascension, the Kingdom of Media had conquered Assyria, then united with the rising kingdom of Persia. In 553 B.C., when Medo-Persia became a military threat to Babylon, Nabonidus moved to Tema in Arabia, a region which had many military advantages. Belshazzar, his eldest, yet inexperienced son ruled as viceroy in Babylon.

Nabonidus was not overly concerned with the inexperience of his son, for Babylon was thought to be impregnable. The city, which was built on both sides of the Euphrates River, had enormous fortified double walls 300 feet high, 80 feet thick, extending 35 feet below ground.

The walls were 60 miles long--15 miles on all four sides--and enclosed an area of some 200 square miles. The outside wall was protected by a wide, deep moat fed by the Euphrates River.

Five brass gates connecting streets to the outside were protected by drawbridges, which were raised at night. The palm-fringed Euphrates ran through the center of the city. Under the river was a tunnel 15 feet wide and 12 feet high, which connected both sides of the city.

The royal palace built by Nebuchadnezzar was likewise considered secure. It stood on the east bank of the Euphrates, one mile south of the north wall where the river entered the city. A 20-foot-thick wall protected it on the south side and a 50-foot-thick wall protected the remaining three sides.

Spanning the north end of the river, between the east and west bank wall, and submerged to a considerable depth below the surface of the water, were two huge, leaved gates of brass. At night the gates were swung shut and secured by large iron bars, which were slid from recesses within the massive walls on each bank of the river. In those days of ancient warfare, the city was impregnable.

The king's devotion to the moon god, Sin, to the neglect of the Babylonian god, Marduk, evidently aroused the priests against his religious program. When Babylonia was threatened by Cyrus' invasion, the pious king collected the various gods surrounding Babylon for safekeeping in Babylon.

The importation of foreign gods into Babylon was a serious threat to the Babylonian priesthood. Marduk, a fearful god who demanded both licentious worship and human sacrifice, might be denounced by these more amiable gods.

Moreover, the priests feared that if Marduk were replaced by a usurper, they might lose their position, and ultimately the control of politics--an unconscionable thought.

"Needless to say", writes historian Dr. James Henry Breasted, "Nabonidus, the Chaldean king of Babylon, was not in favor with the priests, and they assisted in delivering the city to Cyrus."

Recorded on a barrel-shaped clay tablet found in the ruins at Babylon is the priests' version of what happened: "Without battle and without fighting, Marduk made him (Cyrus) enter into his city of Babylon: he spared Babylon tribulation, and Nabonidus, the king who feared him not, he delivered into his (Cyrus') hand."

Although Marduk was given credit for delivering Babylon to the Persians, we realize that this demon-god had no power outside the priesthood. The treasonous priests, fearful of losing their god to a supplanter, and their positions to a new administration of priest-advisors, offered up their city to the Persian army.

The ancient Greek historian Herodotus states that "Cyrus diverted the Euphrates into a new channel, and guided by two deserters, marched by the dry bed into the city while the Babylonians were carousing at the feast of their gods."

Nothing is mentioned by Herodotus of the two underwater leaved gates of brass that spanned the north entrance of the Euphrates--gates that were closed by night and secured by two large iron bars. For the army of Cyrus to enter the city on a dry river bed, the gates had to be unlocked after the river was diverted. Who would have unlocked them but the "two deserters," most likely hired by the priests of Marduk, who were feting the "new" gods of Babylon with Belshazzar, the viceroy-son of Nabonidus.

It is not so difficult to imagine the resentment of the powerful priesthood of Marduk, who feared displacement by another god and his cult. The Babylonian priests found co-conspirators in the Zoroastrian priests of Cyrus. Contacting the Zoroastrians would not have been difficult for they were the world's first missionary priests, roaming the Babylonian countryside for converts.

When the Babylonian priests informed their Zoroastrian counterparts of the scheme to depose Nabonidus, the Zoroastrians carried the proposal to divert the river back to king Cyrus.

In 539 B.C., the Persian army marched on Babylon. Nabonidus was out of the country, possibly in Tema, Arabia. For one year the city was besieged, while workmen dug a new river bed to divert the Euphrates. The night the signal was given to unlock the gates was the night of Belshazzar's party (recorded in Daniel 5).

As the revelry peaked, the two conspirators opened the two leaved gates. The rumble of the heavy iron bars sliding into their recesses could not be heard over the pandemonium of celebration. The Persian army marched into the city on a dry riverbed and took Babylon without a fight. As the priests had recorded on their clay tablets, that night Marduk "spared Babylon tribulation."

The conspiracy to unlock the gates has been prophesied in part by Jeremiah (51:28-30) a half century before, when he foretold that Babylon would be taken by the Medes:

"Prepare the nations for battle against her--the kings of the Medes. The land trembles and writhes, for the Lord's purposes against Babylon stand. Babylon's warriors have stopped fighting . . . they remain in their strongholds . . . the bars of her gates are broken."

The ingenious plot was also prophesied a century earlier by Isaiah. Isaiah 45:1-2 gives greater detail about the "two leaved gates" and the "bars of iron" used to fasten the "gates of brass":

"Thus saith the Lord to his anointed, to Cyrus, whose right hand I have holden, to subdue nations before him; and I will loose the loins of kings, to open before him the two leaved gates; and the gates shall not be shut; I will go before thee, and make the crooked places straight: I will break in pieces the gates of brass, and cut in sunder the bars of iron."

The Hebrew word for "shut" is a primitive root word that figuratively means "to surrender, deliver up, or give over." Therefore the phrase "the gates shall not be shut" actually means, "The gates shall be surrendered."

According to Hislop, there were two Zoroasters. The original is said to have been the first astrologer who developed the Zodiac with horoscopes. He lived thousands of years before a pagan prophet took his name and resurrected Zoroastrianism during the reign of the Persian king, Darius the Great (approx. 500 B.C.).

Zero not only is a part of the pagan deity's name, it is his number as well, symbolized by and circular object. Hence, the sun, moon, and stars became objects of worship in all mystery religions.

The pagans used the circle to illustrate their view of the creation of heaven, earth, and hell, which they referred to collectively as the "three planes of life." Each plane in turn was encompassed by a circle, having within each circle eleven degrees of creation. The first degree was represented by "0," which became the god of that plane.

Through a process of evolution, creation advanced by degrees in each circle until the number "10" was reached, for a total of 11 degrees. Each of the three planes evolved in this manner, totaling 33 degrees to complete all of creation.

BLOODLINES OF THE KING

The first fire worshipers were the Zoroastrians. The Greek historian of the second century A.D., Apollodorus of Athens, wrote in his treatise, "On the Gods," that Ninus was the head of the fire-worshipers. Plato states that the original Zoroaster was a warrior-king. Historians Diodorus Siculus and Justin both claim that Ninus was the first warrior-king. Josephus says that Ninus was Nimrod. Therefore it is likely, that the original Zoroaster, the founder of fire-worship, was none other than Nimrod.

Various researchers and others have come to recognize the fascinating existence of a historical conspiracy to establish a one-world government under a Merovingian descendant.

The story may begin with Merovée, a fifth-century king of the Sicambrians or Germanic Franks (now Germany and France).

Merovée's son, Childeric, practiced witchcraft; his grandson, Clovis I, converted to Roman Catholicism and became the "New Constantine." Some Merovingians claim, however, that Merovée, their forefather, not only had a birthmark in the form of a red cross on his chest, but was a physical descendant of Jesus and Mary the Magdalene. According to this sordid tale, Jesus didn't really die on the cross, but was stolen away from the tomb only to survive and secretly wed Mary the Magdalene (as well as her presumed sister Martha), with whom he then fathered children.

When the Romans temporarily lifted their siege of Jerusalem shortly before its destruction in A.D. 70, Mary the Magdalene fled with her children to France via the Mediterranean Sea, where they eventually married into the royal Frankish family.

Viewing themselves as potentially divine, messianic descendants of King David and Jesus, as well as of the Roman emperors, these Merovingian have therefore sought clandestinely to place their offspring upon the thrones of Europe through intermarriage. (Most of Europe's royal families today are supposedly Merovingian in descent.) But that is not all.

Legend has it that Joseph of Arimathea caught some of the blood of Jesus in the cup from which the Lord drank at the Last Supper with his disciples when His side was pierced by a spear upon the cross. Due to their contact with Jesus' blood, both the cup and the spear, called the "Spear of Longinus" and the Cup of Destiny, have since been associated with certain "magical" powers. The spear, which is said to confer upon its owner the ability to rule the world, but death to anyone who loses it, is currently in the Habsburg Treasure House (a family museum), at Vienna, Austria.

But what about the cup?

Although some accounts hold that Mary the Magdalene took the Cup of Destiny, or the "Holy Grail," with her when she fled to France, others state that Joseph of Arimathea brought it to England, where he and his offspring became the "Guardians of the Grail."

By 1061, France's Roman Catholic Crusaders had captured Jerusalem. Upon doing so, they set Godfroi dé Bouillon, the Merovingian leader of the First Crusade and the Duke of Lorraine, who was directly descended from Dagobert II, Sigisbert IV, and the line of Merovingian "lost kings" and was the grandson of Eustache I and the son of Eustache II, upon the throne; for he claimed Davidic descent.

Later in either 1090 or 1099, Godfroi founded the Order of Sion (Zion), a secret society. In 1111, 1112, or 1118, Hugues dé Payen instituted the Knights Templar (Temple Knights) as a "front organization" for the Order of Zion, and he appointed Godfroi's brother, Baudouin I, as its second grand master (after himself). Subsequently, around 1128, Saint Bernard, abbot of Clairvaux and the age's supposed "chief spokesman for Christendom," declared the Temple Knights to be "the epitome and apotheosis of Christian values." The "Church" then officially recognized and incorporated the Temple Knights as "a religious-military order" of "warrior-monks" and "soldier-mystics," and Hugues dé Payen received the honorary title of grand master of the Temple Knights. In 1188, the Temple Knights separated from the Order of Zion, which then changed its name to the Priory of Sion (Zion). Also in 1188, the Priory of Zion's first grand master, Jean dé Gisors, founded the Rosicrucians.

Originally known as the Order of the Poor Knights of Christ and the Temple of Solomon, the Knights Templar, according to tradition, built their quarters upon the foundations of the ancient temple of Solomon.

Initially headquartered in France, however, the Temple Knights, who are thought to have found and plundered some of the hidden treasures of the destroyed Second Temple, adopted the Merovingian birthmark, a red cross, as their symbol. Introduced into England around 1140, and ultimately threatened by the Roman Catholic Church, they found eventual refuge in Scotland, where the French Templars became the Scottish Rite of Freemasonry.

Rob Simone

The Templars are credited with having instituted a wealthy and influential "international banking system across Europe."

All things considered, the supposed "Protocols of the Elders of Zion," appears not to be a Judaic work, but a modified work of the Priory of Zion, possibly having been altered for public consumption with the complicity of the Illuminati.

From 1188 to the present day, the Priory of Zion has been the "benefactor" of a struggle for dominance between English and French royalty and nobility. Originally a French-English oligarchic order and secret-society, from which came the Knights Templar and the Rosicrucian, its control came to rest largely with the English side, even though a number of its grand masters resided in France.

Jean dé Gisors, the priory's first grand master (1188-1220), for example, was a vassal of the King of England, Henry II, and then Richard I. Note that Henry II was a French Anjou by birth. Marie dé Saint-Clair, the priory's second grand master (1220-1266) and possibly the second wife of Jean dé Gisors, was descended from Henry dé Saint-Clair, Baron of Rosslyn in Scotland, who accompanied Godfroi dé Bouillon on the first Crusade. Rosslyn itself was situated not far from the Templars' major perceptory in Scotland, and Rosslyn Chapel built in the fifteenth century, became mantled with Rose-Croix and Freemasonry legends. The priory's third grand master was Guillaume dé Gisors (1266-1307).

Edouard dé Bar, the priory's fourth grand master (1307-1336), was the grandson of Edward I of England and a nephew of Edward II . . . Edouard's daughter married into the house of Lorraine . . . Edouard was grand-nephew of Guillaume's wife, Iolande dé Bar. Jeanne dé Bar, the priory's fifth grand master (1336-1351), was the elder sister of Edouard and a granddaughter of Edward I of England and a niece of Edward II.

Jeanne seems to have enjoyed extremely cordial relations with the English throne, and to have had similar relations with the king of France. Jean dé Saint-Clair, the priory's sixth grand master (1351-1365), was not only descended from the French houses, but, his grandfather was married to Jeanne dé Bar's aunt.

In other words, he also was a descendant of English royalty. It was during this period, in 1348, that King Edward III founded the Order of the Garter, which, as will be shown later, established itself over the Priory of Zion, the Knights Templar, and the Rosicrucians! Could this be that the Order of the Garter became the heart of the ultimate conspiracy for a New World Order?

René dé Anjou, the priory's ninth grand master (1418-1480), came to hold the titles "Count of Bar" and "King of Jerusalem." René, who seems to have had a particular preoccupation with the Grail, may have played a key role in the Renaissance.

His influence prompted Cosimo dé Medici to embark on a series of ambitious projects destined to transform Western civilization, including the creation of an academy of Pythagorean and Platonic studies. Cosimo's academy quickly generated a multitude of similar institutions throughout the Italian peninsula, which became bastions of Western esoteric tradition. And from them the high culture of the Renaissance began to blossom.

One of René's daughters married Henry VI of England and became a prominent figure in the Wars of the Roses. Henry VI also had Anjou blood. Iolande dé Bar, another of René dé Anjou's daughters, was the priory's tenth grand master (1480-1483).

Louis dé Nevers, the priory's fifteenth grand master (1575-1595), would have functioned in close concert with the treasurer of the military contingent sent by Elizabeth I of England to support the French king. In 1582. Louis was in England consorting with John Dee, the foremost English esotericist of his age.

Robert Fludd, the priory's sixteenth grand master (1595-1637), inherited John Dee's mantle as England's leading exponent of esoteric thought. Fludd warmly endorsed the Rosicrucians, declaring that the highest good was the Magia, Cabala, and Aclhymia of the Brothers of the Rosy Cross.

Enjoying the favor of England's King James I and Charles I, Fludd was among the conclave of scholars who presided over the translation of the (Authorized) King James Bible. (It appears, then, that despite the claims of some, the AKJV translation was not accomplished entirely apart from the influence of heretics and apostates. In fact, it is a noteworthy twist that the British monarchy still holds a copyright on the translation to this day.)

Robert Boyle, the priory's eighteenth grand master (1654-1691), was educated at Eton, where his provost was closely connected with the Rosicrucian entourage. Boyle was among the few English public figures to offer allegiance to the newly crowned Stuarts, and Charles II became patron of the Royal Academy. Boyle's two closest friends were Sir Isaac Newton and John Locke, who shortly after making Boyle's acquaintance, embarked for a lengthy stay in the south of France. Locke is known to have studied the story of the legends according to which the Magdalene brought the Holy Grail to Marseilles.

Sir Isaac Newton, the priory's nineteenth grand master (1691-1727), who claimed descent from Scottish Royalty, was elected President of the Royal Society in 1717.

Newton, who was militantly, albeit quietly, hostile to the idea of the Trinity, and who questioned the divinity of Jesus more than any other scientist of his age, was steeped in Hermetic texts. In addition to personally annotated copies of the Rosicrucian manifestoes, his library included more than a hundred alchemical works.

Newton, whose works reflect interests shared by Masonic figures of the period, was sympathetic to those who stressed the supremacy of gnosis, or direct knowledge, over faith. Moreover, he befriended

Rob Simone

 Jean Desaguliers, who was one of the Royal Society's two curators of experiments, and who became one of the leading figures in the astonishing proliferation of Freemasonry throughout Europe.

Desaguliers presided over the Masonic initiation of Prince Francois, the Duke of Lorraine. Newton's closest friend, Nicolas Fatio dé Duillier, appears to have worked as a spy, usually against Louis XIV of France.

Charles Radclyffe, the priory's twentieth grand master (1727-1746), an illegitimate grandson of King Charles II, was created an Earl of Derwentwater by King James II. As such, he devoted much of his life to the Stuart cause. Charles V dé Lorraine, the priory's twenty-first grand master (1746-1780), was probably exposed to a Jacobite influence; for his father had offered protection and refuge at Bar-le-Duc to the exiled Stuarts.

Charles was Austrian field marshal in the eighteenth century, and brother-in-law to the Empress Maria Theresa. His court resembled that of René de Anjou, his ancestor and another prominent Merovingian.

Perhaps relevant, Maximilian dé Lorraine, the priory's twenty-second grand master (1780-1801), seems to have acted through cultural figures, as well as through certain of his own numerous siblings-- Marie Caroline, for instance, who as queen of Naples and Sicily was largely responsible for the spread of Freemasonry in those domains.

 Charles Nodier, the priory's twenty-third grand master (1801-1844), appears to be the first of the priory's grand master lacking noble blood. Nevertheless, he published a seditious tract in London in opposition to Napoleon and claimed involvement in two separate plots against Napoleon.

Victor Hugo, the priory's twenty-fourth grand master (1844-1885), whose father maintained very cordial relations with the conspirators involved in the plot against the French emperor, was a fervent disciple of Charles Nodier. Like Newton, he was militantly anti-Trinitarian and repudiated Jesus' divinity. He was immersed all his life in esoterica, in Gnostic, Cabalistic, and hermetic thought. And he is known to have been connected with a so-called Rose-Croix order.

John Cocteau, the priory's twenty-sixth grand master (1918), decorated such churches as Notre Dame dé France in London.

From the above documentation, it seems clear that the Priory of Sion has in fact been more a historical tool of the English monarchy and nobility than of the French.

It is of significant interest, therefore, that the Priory of Sion, the Temple Knights, and the Rosicrucians, all of which ultimately derive from the earlier Order of Zion, together gave rise to English and French Freemasonry.

Moreover, in 1848, as will be more fully documented later, the Order of the Garter became the major control point from which the English monarchy exercised its global influence.

Recall that Godfroi dé Bouillon, a Merovingian crusader, founded the Order of Zion in either 1090 or 1099. Upon Godfroi's death in 1100, Baudouin I (Baldwin I) assumed the title "King of Jerusalem." Following him, Baldwin II, Baldwin III, Amalric I, Baldwin IV, Baldwin V, and several others, all of whom were of Merovingian descent, held the title.

Eventually it passed to Emperor Charles V dé Lorraine, who, as a descendant of the Merovingian Hildegarde and the twenty-first grand master of the Priory of Zion, married Eleonore Marie von Habsburg, daughter of Emperor Ferdinand III. The Habsburg (also spelled "Hapsburg") dynasty, which descends separately from Merovée through Alex, the sister of Godfroi and Badouin I, has held it ever since. Currently, Otto Von Habsburg of Austria, the titular Duke of Lorraine who under better circumstances would have been called Emperor of Austria, Apostolic King of Hungary, and Holy Roman Emperor, holds the title, while King Juan Carlos of Spain claims it.

King Juan likewise descends from Eleonore Marie and Charles V, who, as the grandson of the Spanish Isabella, also ruled Spain as King Charles I.

My research has connected the beliefs of the Priory of Zion and its offspring with ancient Zoroastrianism, as well as with the spiritual "enlightenment" represented by the "seeing eye" of the Illuminati, which is depicted in the capstone at the top of their pyramidal "Great Seal" on the U.S. dollar bill (arguably the world's most important currency).

We may also connect them with the modern New Age Movement. Interestingly, from 188 to 1306, the Priory of Sion supposedly also called itself "Omnus," a name that figures in Zoroastrian thought and in Gnostic texts, where it is synonymous with the principle of light, although Masonic tradition would have us believe that the name derives from an ancient Egyptian sage and mystic who conferred a red cross upon his initiates, giving rise to the first Rosicrucian.

Relics and Symbols

The Spear of Longinus, which had pierced the side of Christ, passed into the hands of Constantine, who wielded the "serpent powers" of the Spear to rise to the throne of the Roman Empire (A.D. 307-337).

Constantine held it to his breast before the assembled Church fathers, when he declared himself to be the "Thirteenth Apostle." It is the opinion of some scholars that Constantine, in A.D. 313, not Peter, was made the first Pope. In A.D. 315, he made Roman Catholicism the mandatory state religion. He also carried the Spear with him when he staked out the boundaries of Constantinople, his new capital city.

When he moved his throne from Rome in 324, he split the Roman Empire. In the years that followed, the Eastern Orthodox Church became strong while the Roman Church faltered.

Around A.D. 500, the Roman Church made a pact with Clovis, the King of the Franks and grandson of Merovée, to be the new emperor of the Holy Roman Empire.

With the assassination of Dagobert II in 679, the Merovingians were replaced by the Carolingian dynasty. Pepin II (Pepin the Fat) engineered the death of Dagobert and passed the power of the kingdom on to his son, the famous Charles Martel. Charles was also known as Carl the Hammer, from whom the Carolingian dynasty derived its name.

Charles Martel is considered to be one of the most heroic figures in French history. He assembled a great army of all the kingdoms of Europe and led the armies against the Arabs in the Battle of Tours in 752, one of the great battles to decide the fate of the world. It was this battle that determined whether Europe would be Christian or Muslim. By virtue of Charles' victory, he has become known as the "savior of Christendom."

It was said that the new ruler possessed the "Spear of Longinus," and used it as a symbol of his power when he drove the invading Muslims from the continent of Europe. His grandson, the famous Charlemagne, used the Spear as a symbol of his political power. He kept it with him night and day, for he believed it to have magical powers.

Charlemagne, known as the father of the Holy Roman Empire, came to the throne in 800. He was not only the King of France, but also the crowned emperor of the Roman Empire. He founded his whole dynasty on the possession of the Spear and its legend of world historic destiny--a legend which attracted the greatest scholars in all Europe to serve the power of the Holy Roman Empire. Charlemagne fought 46 campaigns with assurance of victory through the power of the Spear.

The legendary spear was said to have given him clairvoyant faculties through which he discovered the burial place of Saint James in Spain, and uncanny powers to anticipate future events.

Throughout his life, Charlemagne lived and slept within reach of the Spear. After the victory of his last campaign, he accidentally let the Spear fall from his hands.

His soldiers believed that the dropping of the Spear was an omen of his impending death. Such was said to be the occult powers of the Spear. In the years that followed it was passed from one emperor of the Holy Roman Empire to another.

Around 1140, the Knights Templar arrived in Jerusalem. They were given living quarters in the palace of King Baudouin on the Temple site. Though there is no historical proof, it is believed that they spent the next nine years digging--digging up the buried treasure of the ancient Jewish Temple.

In 1953 a copper scroll was found in a cave near the Dead Sea which told of a fabulous Temple treasure--estimated at more than 138 tons of gold and silver which had been buried by the Jewish priesthood in 64 locations before the Romans destroyed the Temple in A.D. 70. Twenty-four of those hordes of gold and silver were buried under the Temple Mountain. It is believed that the Knights Templar plundered the treasure of the Temple and took it back to Europe. After nine years in Jerusalem, the Templars returned to Europe wealthy beyond belief.

In the years following, they built castles all over Europe and became famous as the guardians of the Holy Grail. It is believed that the Priory of Sion organized the Knights Templar to excavate the Temple site in hopes of finding more of the treasure of the Temple. Evidently they were successful, for they instituted an international banking system across Europe and had the resources to loan gold to kings and governments.

The Knights Templar soon broke away from their allegiance to the Bishop of Rome and became an arrogant organization aloof from all recognized authority. They refused to be subject to kings or popes. Those international bankers also invented a method by which they could transfer gold from one city to another or from one bank to another, simply by writing a note on a piece of paper. Today, we call it writing checks.

The secret purpose for the Knights Templar, however, was to preserve the Merovingian bloodline in hopes of one day establishing a world government and putting their king upon the throne--a king who could claim to be the offspring of Jesus Christ and Mary Magdalene.

The Knights Templar wore white uniforms, each having a large red cross on the mantle. Legends were told of their exploits. They were the guardians of the Holy Grail, the so-called cup from which Jesus drank at the Last Supper, and of the Grail family, the bloodline of the Magdalene.

In 1168, there was a split between the Order of Sion and the Knights Templar. Only the year before, the Knights had lost a battle over Jerusalem and their Grand Master was accused of treason. From that time the days of the Knights Templar were numbered.

The King of France tried to destroy the Knights Templar and confiscate their treasure in the early 1300s. Between 1303 and 1305, Philip IV, King of France, engineered the kidnapping and death of Pope Boniface VIII and the murder by poison of his successor, Pope Benedict XI. In 1305 King Philip managed to secure the election of his own candidate, the Archbishop of Bordeaux, to the vacant papal throne.

The new pontiff took the name Clement V and together with Philip organized the infamous "Inquisition" in an effort to destroy the power and influence of the Knights Templar--and especially the Merovingian bloodline that hung like a cloud over the Roman Church. Another main objective was to confiscate the treasures of the Temple.

On October 13, 1307, all Templars in France were arrested--including their Grand Master, Jacques dé Molay. The king also tried to locate the treasure of the Templars, but the treasure could not be found. In March 1314, Jacques dé Molay, the Grand Master of the Knights Templar, and Geoffrey dé Charney (owner of the shroud, today called the Shroud of Turin), were burned at the stake. From that point on, the Knights seemed to vanish from the stage of history. Nevertheless, the order continued to exist.

The French Templars found a refuge in Scotland, where the group maintained itself as a coherent body for at least the next 400 years. They eventually developed into an organization called the Scottish Rite.

Also, over the centuries, the symbol of the skull and crossbones has been connected with the Knights Templar. The symbol was used hundreds of years ago by the pirates on the high seas. In more recent times it became a symbol of warning used on bottles of poison.

Many European tombs of the Templars contain the symbol of the skull and crossbones. It has been suggested that the original skull and crossbones may have been those of Mary Magdalene.

By 1789, the legends surrounding the ancient Knights Templar pictured them as illumined alchemists, magi, and sages--veritable supermen endowed with an awesome arsenal of arcane power and knowledge. They were regarded as heroes and martyrs.

The death of Jacques dé Molay at the hands of King Philip was never forgotten. During the French Revolution, as the head of King Louis XVI fell beneath the guillotine, a man leaped onto the scaffold, dipped his hand in the monarch's blood, flung it out over the surrounding throng, and cried, "Jacques dé Molay, thou art revenged!"

The mystique surrounding the Knights Templar has not diminished. There have been a few contemporary organizations, which claimed to possess a pedigree from the ancient organization.

Certain Masonic lodges have adopted the grade of Templar, as well as rituals supposedly descended from the original order.

In the United States, young men are admitted into the De Molay Society--a fraternal organization--most without adequate knowledge of the origin of the name. It was taken from Jacques dé Molay, the 14th-century Grand Master of the Knights Templar.

In the Mormon temple, certain rites are performed which are identical to Masonic rites. Mormonism also has a philosophical connection to the order of the ancient Templars.

In the last century, Helena Blavatsky, founder of Theosophy, spoke of an esoteric wisdom tradition running back through the Rosicrucians to the Knights Templar. The teaching of Helena Blavatsky can best be seen in the New Age Movement today.

Toward the end of the 19th century it is alleged a sinister Order of Templars was established in Germany and Austria employing the swastika as one of its emblems. At first it was known as the Thule Society but later changed its name to the Nazi Party.

The Order of the Knights Templar was, at first, only a front organization for a more secretive group known as the Priory of Sion, whose real purpose was to capture the wealth of the world, establish their own world government, and introduce a Merovingian king to sit upon a throne in Jerusalem. They are said to be the true possessors of the Temple treasury and the behind the scenes controllers of the world's currencies. There are many cryptic references in popular culture to this theory.

The classical definition of the world's oldest secret fraternal organization (or society), the Freemasons, is that it is a system of "Morality veiled in Allegory."

It is a system of three ritual initiations, or degrees, based on the medieval Stonemason's guilds, guarded by blood oaths and founded on the principles of the fatherhood of God and the brotherhood of Man.

Stonemasons were employed in the building of the great cathedrals of Europe. They formed unions and were a respected part of the community. The pagan symbols of gargoyles, demons, and unicorns found on the cathedrals, gives a hint of their occultist ties. Perhaps, the first printing of the name "Mason" can be found in the poem "Muses Trinity" by a Rosicrucian named Anderson.

"For we be brethren of the Rosy Cross and we have the Mason word and second sight."

Second sight is paranormal activity or ESP (extra sensory perception). During the Reformation, and after Luther's posting of the 95 theses arguing against many Roman Catholic practices on the cathedral door in Wittenberg, Germany, cathedral building ground to a halt. It was Luther's argument against the selling of indulgences that was to blame.

The Stonemason's rule of disallowing members in their guild if they were rich was soon abolished. Wealthier members of the guild were known as Speculative Masons.

Modern Freemasonry (also known as the "Masonic Association") was established when Rosicrucianism united all English lodges under one Grand (or Mother) Lodge on July 24, 1717, at Appletree Tavern in London.

Freemasonry spread through England like wildfire. Hundred of lodges were in operation in less than ten years, spreading to Germany, France, and the rest of Europe in short order.

Freemasonry had come to France in 1725, but by 1772 the organization had split into two groups, one of which had become known as the Grand Orient Lodge of Freemasonry.

The Grand Orient Lodge spread quickly throughout the entirety of France so that by 1789, there was about 600 lodges all over France, as compared to some 104 in 1772. Members of the Grand Orient were also active in government, as 447 of the 605 members of the estates General, France's parliament, were members.

To most students of the conspiracy, the modern day manifestation began on May 1st, 1776, with the founding of the "Illuminati," by Adam Weishaupt, a Jesuit priest, and a professor of Canon Law at Inglestott University in Bavaria, today part of Germany. Weishaupt's organization spread quickly, especially among fellow intellectuals at his university. There is some evidence that Weishaupt had become affiliated with secret societies before he founded the Illuminati. It is unclear exactly what influenced Weishaupt's motives.

The basic philosophy that was being offered to the prospective member of the Illuminati was a reversal of the traditional philosophy taught by the church and the educational system.

It has been summarized by Weishaupt himself as follows, "Man is not bad except as he is made so by arbitrary morality; he is bad because religion, the state, and bad examples pervert him. When at last, reason becomes the religion of men, then will the problem be solved."

There is reason to believe that Weishaupt's contempt of religion started on July 1, 1773, when Pope Clement XIV forever annulled and extinguished the Jesuit order. The Pope's action was in response to pressure from France, Spain, and Portugal, which independently had come to the conclusion that the Jesuits were meddling in the affairs of the state and were therefore enemies of the government. Pope Clemet's action was short-lived though, as Pope Pius VII, in August 1814, reinstated the Jesuits to all of their former rights and privileges.

Nesta Webster, one of the major researchers into the Illuminati has summarized their goals as follows:

1. Abolition of monarchy and all ordered government.

2. Abolition of private property.

3. Abolition of inheritance.

4. Abolition of patriotism (nationalism).

5. Abolition of the family (for example, of marriage and all morality, and the institution of communal education of children).

6. Abolition of all religion.

In 1777, Weishaupt was initiated into the Masonic Order, the Lodge Theodore of Good Counsel, in Munich, Germany. His purpose in joining was not to become part of this benevolent order, but to infiltrate it and then to control it altogether. In fact, the Masons held an international congress at Wilhelmsbad, Germany, in July 1782, and Illuminism was injected into Freemasonry by indoctrinating the Masonic leaders.

It was in the French Grand Orient Freemasonic Lodges that the Illuminati took root. However, the secrecy of the Illuminati was soon broken in 1783 when four professors of the Mariannan Academy were summoned before the court of inquiry and questioned on the Illuminati.

The Bavarian government had discovered the philosophies and purposes of the Illuminati and, more importantly, its desire to overthrow the Bavarian government.

Hearings were held, and the government abolished the order. But, discovery of the organization was perhaps, a blessing in disguise. The members fled the persecution of the Bavarian government and they took the Illuminati with them, establishing new societies all over Europe and America.

Rob Simone

The Bavarian government countered this expansion by warning other European governments about the exact purposes of the Illuminati, but the rulers of Europe refused to listen.

Those decisions would later come back to haunt these governments as Nesta Webster observed, "the extravagance of the scheme therein propounded, rendered it unbelievable and the rulers of Europe refusing to take Illuminist seriously, put it aside as a foolish fancy."

There was one head of state who did take the warnings seriously, George Washington. Below is an actual hand-written letter penned on September 25, 1798 in which he talks about the Illuminati influence on America.

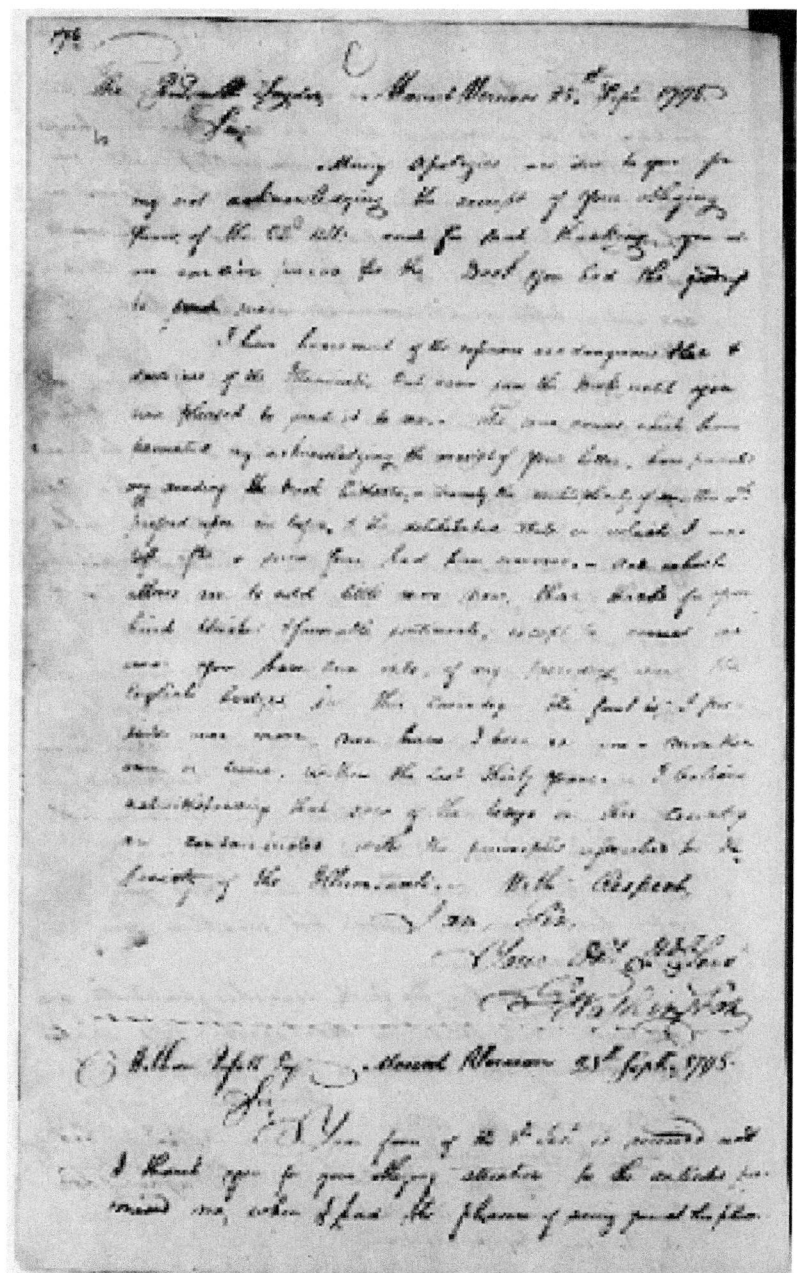

"It was not my intention to doubt that the doctrines of the Illuminati ...has not spread into the United States, on the contrary, no one is more satisfied of this fact than I am"

Today, we can only speculate what Washington would conclude of the concerns in his letter in today's modern society.

Since the era of the Sumerian Kings, through Colonial times up to today, the ancient teachings and the societies who practice them, continue to influence politics, the economy, and world events. Ω

Biography

After more than 10 years as an independent researcher and research analyst into many areas of unexplained phenomenon, Rob Simone earned a legal degree, moved to Sedona Arizona in the late 1990's and began working for the civil activist organization, C.A.U.S. Citizens Against UFO Secrecy.

Rob worked directly with the director, Peter Gersten Esq. C.A.U.S. was featured regularly on Art Bell and countless other radio and TV programs for the organization's use of the legal system to expose the government's secrecy and cover up of the extra-terrestrial phenomenon.

Rob became the world's first "para-normal para-legal" collecting affidavits, eyewitness testimony and photographic evidence for FOIA (Freedom of Information Act) requests for various lawsuits brought against the D.O.D. (Dept of Defense) and the Federal Government.

This involved liaisons with many other research groups, coordination of media, and direct contact with witnesses, government insiders and high-level military officials whose stories can now be told.

One of these lawsuits was appealed all the way to the Supreme Court, and is still used today as a legal precedent.

Then, a 3 year trip around the world to the most mystical, sacred and powerful places on earth, investigating cultural and historical links to the para-normal and extra-terrestrial components of many ancient civilizations and belief systems.

This included gathering first-hand accounts from indigenous peoples and tribal elders of the unexplained and metaphysical aspects of their social and religious constructs, both past and present.

A special focus of Rob's research is on the E.T./supernatural aspects of Islam and the origins of the Holy Koran.

Rob Simone is an award-winning media personality and accomplished TV and radio producer. In addition, Rob has authored 2 books and is a featured writer for national magazines.

Rob has hosted radio shows in Australia, Katmandu Nepal on HBC FM, and currently in London England on 104.4 FM, and was recently included in FATE Magazine's "Top 100 Ufologists" list along with Dan Aykoyd and Steven Spielberg.

Rob is Executive Director of Universal Sound and Light Productions and founder of **A.I.R.,** The Association of Independent Researchers. Rob now lives in Los Angeles where he continues to produce radio and television projects related to the field. Rob has been featured in UFO Magazine, FATE Magazine, FOX News, Japan's Nippon TV, China's CCTV, Channel 4 U.K., and recently on the 2-hour History Channel program "Decoding The Past."

Rob Simone's Lecture Topics include:

THE EXTRA-TERRESRIAL ENCOUNTERS OF THE ABORIGINAL ABDUCTEES AND THE 2012 PARADIGM

During his travels, Rob gathered first-hand accounts from indigenous peoples and tribal elders in the Outback of Australia of ancient and recent E.T. abductions, UFO contacts and future planetary earth changes.

Having lived in Australia for a year, Rob explored the tribal traditions and artwork of the Aboriginals to decode the inter-dimensional legacy of their knowledge and culture. The Elders speak of a future "Dream Time," of dramatic human changes that correlate directly with the 2012 Mayan Calendar cycle.

This includes stunning pictures and video of the most up close and the best documented evidence ever collected.

INTERNATIONAL UFOLOGY
A GLOBAL PERSPECTIVE TO A GALACTIC PHENOMENON

The E.T. and Para-normal research from the Asian, Middle Eastern, Aboriginal and Muslim perspective, which chronicles Rob's 3-year odyssey through 25 different countries gathering first-hand accounts from indigenous peoples and tribal elders of unexplained and paranormal components of ancient civilizations and the historical links to the major religions and belief systems.
This lecture will take you into the extra-terrestrial aspects of the Islamic culture from the earliest references of alien abductions to the "engineering" of the human race.

This lecture includes startling new information about Saddam Hussein's deep involvement with the occult and alien aspects of the Muslim religion and his connection to the "stargates" of the Sumerian kings.

Rob decodes the secrets of the true encounters behind the sacred texts of the Holy Koran.

This presentation will take a special look at the Australian aboriginals and their "star people" legends from their distant past, as well as their current contacts. Also, a revealing look at the famous Turkish Air Force- UFO "dogfight" incident. The most up to date and comprehensive overview of this phenomenon
including stunning artwork, photographs and video from around the world.

THE MAYAN CALENDAR
2012 HUMAN EVOLUTION PARADIGM

The lecture explains the origins and complexities of the Mayan Calendar and its inherent natural rhythms and how the 13-moon, 28 day calendar enhances our health, consciousness and synchronicity.

Our modern calendar is an arbitrary means of calculating days and years and is not in alignment with the true movements of the planets and the sun. This causes everyone to disconnect from the natural order of the universe.

Turning our backs on the movement and alignments
of the planets, something that all of the ancient civilizations
held dear, causes us to be off center in our day-to-day and year-to-year planning.

Our understanding of ourselves and our relationship with time itself, hangs in the balance.

THE TAO OF UFOLOGY

The ancient race on Mars discovered from 6000 year old Taoist texts, and the Billy Meier - Pleiadian parallels.

Dramatic photographic evidence of artificial structures and agricultural remains on the Lunar and Martian surface.

This Lecture includes an overview of the ancient writings of Chinese Taoist masters and the earliest globe of the earth ever discovered.

THE COSMIC PARADIGM OF SACRED PLACES AND ISLAMIC UFOLOGY

This workshop will take you into the extraterrestrial aspects of the Islamic culture from the earliest references of alien abductions, the "engineering" of the human race, the secrets of King Solomon's connection with beings from other worlds.

Rob will decode the secrets of the true encounters behind the sacred texts of the Holy Koran. This lecture includes startling new information about Saddam Hussein's deep involvement with the occult and alien aspects of the Muslim religion and his connection to the "stargates" of the Sumerian kings.

Also, a revealing look at the famous Turkish Air Force - UFO "dogfight" incident, the mysterious anomaly photographed over the Dome of the Rock in Jerusalem, and the amazing Annunaki Artifact. This presentation will also take a special look at the Australian aboriginals and their "star people" legends from their distant past, as well as their current contacts.

This will be an up-to-date and comprehensive overview of these cases, including astonishing artwork, photographs and video from around the world.

UFOLOGY 101

This lecture explores the basics of this "emerging science."
Rob traces back UFO and "star visitors" evidence from
30,000 years ago from cave paintings, renaissance artwork,
Jesus and the Virgin Mary connections,
through the current era of Roswell and the National Security State.

With actual audio clips of Presidents Ford, Jimmy Carter and Dick Cheney talking about UFOs! The lecture incorporates stunning pictures and footage of never before seen UFO footage from around the world.

This lecture provides deep understanding of this subject historically, politically and culturally

A TRAVELLOG FROM A JOURNEY AROUND THE WORLD A LOOK INTO THE MOST FASCINATING PLACES ON EARTH

A "mainstream" first hand account of an adventure around the world, to the most famous and unusual places on Earth.

Includes amazing photographs and audio recordings.

This lecture describes the experiences and first hand reports of interesting experiences with people of the Middle East, Asia, India, Nepal, Australia, The Philippines, China, Japan, and Europe. In a revealing way, this lecture highlights the most interesting aspects of these countries and regions.

Also included are many practical ideas and information for the would-be traveler to be safe, see more, and do it all for much less while having more fun.

Includes photographs (never before published) from around the world.

THE SPIRITUALITY OF DISCLOSURE

The overall spiritual implications of extra-terrestrial contact and its impact on the global perspective.

The shifting into a larger reality and how to reconcile this new awareness with our existing faith.

The delay of "Official Disclosure" has slowed the spiritual development of millions of people for far too long.

True disclosure begins with personal acceptance and understanding of our place in the universe and what that means to the survival and evolution of the Earth and of humanity.

This includes spectacular pictures and video of the most up close and best-documented cases ever collected.

THE RADIO CAREER OF AN INTERNATIONAL BROADCASTER

The lecture describes a radio careers in Australia, Kathmandu and London. The unusual and wild stories of radio stations in foreign lands. The bizarre situations and political unrest in developing countries.

This includes a visual travellog covering Asia, India, Nepal, the Middle East, the U.K., Turkey, Greece, Sweden, Denmark and more. This is a first hand account of travels to the most interesting places on the earth!

UFOs IN THE HEADLINES – Real Reporting On A Real Phenomenon

Lost until now, the hard-hitting headlines from the mainstream press from the 1950's onward of the biggest and most compelling UFO/E.T news stories ever published.

The history of the E.T. presence from a journalistic perspective. This includes recent national news and archival material from Rob's new book - "UFOs IN THE HEADLINES.

This also includes new revelations of the 1952 Washington D.C. events, a dramatic UFO encounter during N.A.T.O's Operation Mainbrace and public statements about UFOs by Author C. Clarke and the Duke of Edinburgh and archival and recent UFO footage.

Products: available at www.RobSimone.com

Archive Interview Box Sets Volume 1 & 2   10 audio CD's Each

www.RobSimone.com

The Broadcast Box Set Vol. 1

5 Interviews on 10 Audio CDs

Major Ed Dames   David Icke

William Henry

Jim Marrs   Michael Cremo

Mind-Blowing Interviews with NO commercials

www.RobSimone.com

JIM MARRS   The global secret society network from ancient times to now and beyond

DAVID ICKE   The highlights of his books "The Biggest Secret", "Tales From The Time Loop", and "Children of the Matrix" - also the Illuminati, mind control the and the solutions

WILLIAM HENRY   Stargates, Saddam Hussein, secrets of Sumeria and the 2012 connection

MICHAEL CREMO   The real history of Earth, lost civilizations, out of place artifacts and the extreme antiquity of man

MAJOR ED DAMES   The most controversal remote viewer – UFO's E.T.'s Rods and much more

Rob hosts a highly rated in-depth radio program on 104.4 FM in London England where he talks with the worlds leading authors and researchers

www.**RobSimone**.com

The Broadcast Box Set Vol. 2

5 Interviews on 10 Audio CDs

Zecharia Sitchin   **Nick Redfern**

Al Bielek

Dr. David Morehouse   **Larry Hunter**

Mind-Blowing Interviews with NO commercials

www.**RobSimone**.com

ZECHARIA SITCHIN	Rob and Zecharia recall common experiences in Turkey and their "discovering" the same artifact which could depict an ancient Annunaki astronaut and craft dated to 2500 B.C. (picture included)
AL BIELEK	Al was on the U.S.S Eldridge on the 28th of October in 1943 when the bizarre time travel gateway was opened using Tesla technology sending Al on an incredible adventure through time. In-depth information on the Philadelphia Experiment, Martian bases and the Montauk Project
DR. DAVID MOREHOUSE	Author of "Psychic Warrior" David was trained by the military to be a remote viewer in operation "Sunstreak". For the first time he talks in great detail about his involvement in clandestine covert military operations, government cover-ups, the Gulf War syndrome, the C.I.A. drug trade and the capabilities and limitations of R.V.
NICK REDFERN	Author of "Strange Secrets" and "A Covert Agenda" Nick has uncovered startling de-classified government documents which proves the U.S.and U.K. governments involvement in UFO's, abductions, crop circles, strange animal deaths and Noah's Ark !
LARRY HUNTER	The Secrets of the Pyramids, their real age and purpose, secret underground passageways under the Giza Plateau and the discovery of the tomb Osiris! Also a shocking expose' of Dr. Zahi Hawass

Rob hosts a highly rated in-depth radio program on 104.4 FM in London England where he talks with the worlds leading authors and researchers

A Complete Overview of the UFO Phenomenon From Ancient Times to the Modern Age

Rob decodes the symbols and artwork through the ages pointing to ongoing E.T. contact from 30,000 year old cave paintings and images from Europe, China, Japan, Egypt, Australia and much more. PLUS audio clips of 3 presidents and Dick Cheney talking about UFOs! Also STUNNING footage from around the world, the newest, clearest footage ever

Lecture DVD – running time: 55Min.

www.RobSimone.com

Mankind's most carefully guarded secret revealed!

Filmed in high definition
Running time: 96 min. universal format

Astounding revelations by the world's foremost authorities.
Winner of the People's Choice EBE Award 2007

www.RobSimone.com

Sacred Places and International Ufology Lecture DVD - with Paranormal Expert - Rob Simone

Running time: approx. 1 – ½ hrs.

This workshop lecture DVD examines the E.T., UFO and Para-normal research from the Asian, Middle Eastern, Aboriginal and Muslim perspective, which chronicles Rob's 3 year odyssey through 25 different countries gathering first-hand accounts from indigenous peoples and tribal elders of unexplained and paranormal components of ancient civilizations and the historical links to the major religions and belief systems. This lecture includes stunning artwork, photographs and video from around the world! This lecture will take you into the extra-terrestrial aspects of the Islamic culture. This presentation will take a special look at the Australian aboriginals and their "star people" legends from their distant past, as well as their current contacts. Rob presents his research into the Crop Circle enigma and explores fascinating new images and information about the science of this mystery. Also, a revealing look at the famous Turkish Air Force - UFO "dogfight" incident.

www.RobSimone.com

Real Reporting on a Real Phenomenon

by Rob Simone

Lost until now, the hard-hitting headlines from the mainstream press from the 1950's onward of the biggest and most compelling UFO/E.T news stories ever published. This includes new revelations of the 1952 Washington D.C. events, a dramatic UFO encounter during N.A.T.O.'s Operation Mainbrace and public statements about UFOs by Author C. Clarke and the Duke of Edinburgh.

In this book Rob Simone takes a closer look at UFOs in mainstream media. From 1950 to the present day, this book highlights over 300 photographs of REAL newspaper articles about UFOs from over 7 different countries, from such newspapers as the New York Times and the Washington Post and much more.

BIG 8-1/2 x 11 inch "coffee table" format – now available.

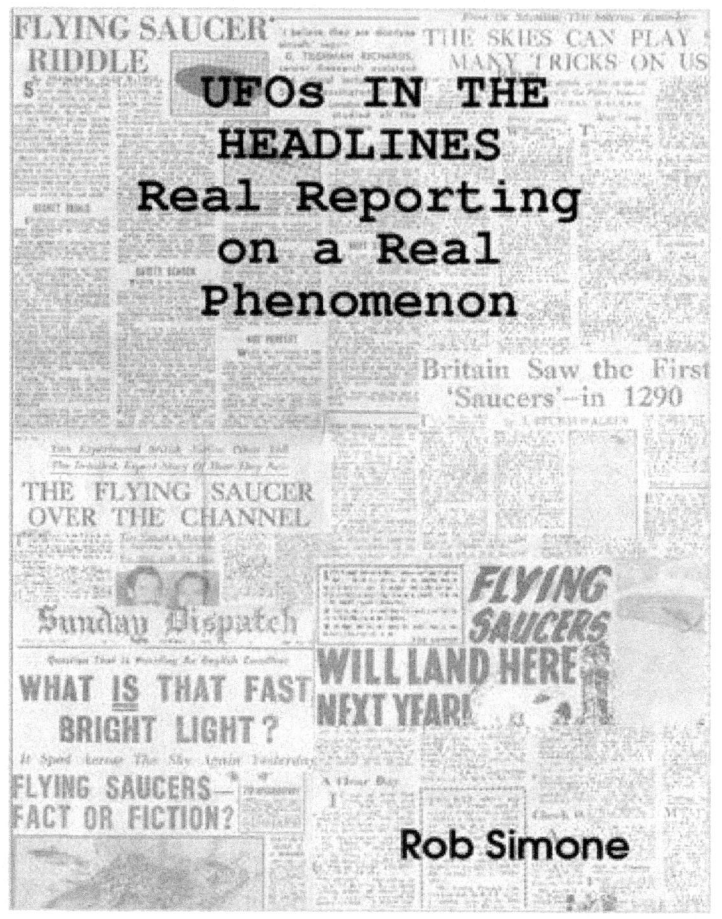

Beyond All Borders

by Rob Simone

Rob has just completed his manuscript "**Beyond All Borders**" which is the continuation of this book, and contains all of Rob's research and global adventures.

This is the true account of Rob's experiences moving to Sedona, working with the civil activist organization C.A.U.S. Citizens Against UFO Secrecy. CAUS was the first organization to bring lawsuits against the U.S. Government in an attempt to release classified documents relating to the UFO cover-up.

Then an around the world adventure that would go through the Outback of Australia, the Himalayas in Nepal, through Asia, into the Middle East, to the Great Pyramids at Giza, rediscovering the Ark of the Covenant, exploring mystical dimensions and meeting the Dalai Lama.

Rob traveled through 25 countries interviewing indigenous peoples and tribal elders about the unexplained and paranormal components of ancient civilizations and their historical links to major religions and belief systems. There is a special focus on the folk legends and supernatural aspects of Islam and the Holy Koran.

This included surviving dangerous battles in the Israeli/Palestinian conflict and the warring factions in Yemen. There is also a compilation of interviews from the past six years of Rob's broadcasting career in Australia, Nepal and London. This includes highlights of the most amazing moments in talk radio ever.

This new book is over 350 pages and is the product of over 10 years of research and travels to the most mysterious and sacred places on earth.

Publisher inquiries welcome

UFOs
Crop Circles and
the Mayan Calendar

A Collection of Articles

By
Rob Simone

Headroom Publishing

Box 9 Lafayette Hill, PA 19444

(614) 748-9471

© Copyright 2007 – Rob Simone

UFOs Crop Circles and the Mayan Calendar

A Collection of Articles

By
Rob Simone

Headroom Publishing

Box 9 Lafayette Hill, PA 19444

(614) 748-9471

© Copyright 2007 – Rob Simone

Printed in Dunstable, United Kingdom